D1341040

THE FORTY DAYS

THE FORTY DAYS

Studies in the last six weeks of our Lord's earthly life, from
Calvary and Easter to the Ascension

by

GEOFFREY R. KING

He showed Himself alive after His passion by
many infallible proofs, being seen of them
forty days.

HENRY E. WALTER LTD.
26 GRAFTON ROAD, WORTHING
& LONDON W.C.2

First Edition 1949
New Edition Revised and Reset 1960

Made and Printed in England for
Henry E. Walter, Ltd., 26 Grafton Road, Worthing,
by Latimer, Trend & Co., Ltd., Plymouth

FOREWORD

by

Rev. Professor James S. Stewart, D.D.

"THE word of the Cross", writes Karl Barth, "is understood and delivered in the sense of Scripture and the Creed, namely, as 'power of God' (1 Cor. i. 18) only where it proclaims in all its awful gravity the joy and the peace of the Easter message." It is astonishing that so many books on the Atonement have been content to stop short at the Cross, or have brought in the Resurrection only as an epilogue, an appendix to the story of the sacrifice of Jesus. It cannot be said too emphatically that there is no salvation for this distracted and bewildered world in a theology that ends at Calvary. "If Christ be not raised, your faith is vain."

This is the apostolic emphasis throughout. The theme was "Jesus and the Resurrection" (Acts xvii. 18). This was the message which, beginning from Jerusalem, crossed mountains, traversed continents, bridged oceans, penetrated strongholds of idolatry and corruption, to bring hope to the disillusioned, liberty to the captives, and victory to the defeated. The darkness of paganism was scattered by the light from an empty tomb.

Do not let us suppose that that light was simply or mainly a new argument for immortality. The New Testament is not primarily concerned with the questions which occupied Plato and later philosophers. It is conspicuously uninterested in mere survival as such. Immortality is Greek: Resurrection is Christian. In other words, Easter is the triumph of God over death indeed, but more than that—over all the principalities and powers that bedevil history and bind men in the vicious circle of their own iniquity. It is the assurance that in grappling with the mystery of evil we are fighting an already defeated enemy.

7

This is the inner revolutionary meaning of the Easter morning Hallelujahs.

It is because this book recalls us so decisively to the centrality of the Resurrection that I now warmly commend it. The forty days of which its title tells take us beyond all partial truths of revelation and confront us with the actual presence of the Kingdom and the King. They bring us indeed to the place where we meet the living God, travelling in the greatness of His strength, mighty to save. I trust that through these pages many may encounter Christ as truly as Thomas did in the upper room, or Saul on the Damascus road in the days of long ago.

J. S. STEWART.

New College, Edinburgh.
  January, 1960.

CONTENTS

NOTE TO PRESENT EDITION

So many letters have come from all round the continents expressing pleasure and helpfulness that it seemed well to publish a second edition, the demand steadily continuing. I was advised to retain the spoken style and even the contemporary allusions. So here is the little book as before, save only that it is now a paper-back and no longer cloth bound.

The late Dr. Frank W. Boreham wrote a most gracious Foreword to the first edition; and for this one my good friend the publisher has secured an equally kindly word from Professor James S. Stewart, one of the living heroes of every preacher, for which I am very grateful.

The picture on the dust jacket is Eugene Burnand's masterpiece of Peter and John running to the Sepulchre on Easter morning—surely one of the immortal portrait-studies of all time. That wide-eyed wonder and thrill of devotion I have sought to recapture in these pages.

I have assumed the traditional " Good Friday ", though I have great respect for the theory that our Lord was crucified on the Wednesday, this providing the three days and three nights. I realize, too, that there is a case for 1 Peter 3: 19 referring to His resurrection spirit-body, and that there is another well-supported school of thought regarding the " sons of God " of Genesis 6 (pp. 24, 25).

My friend, Principal John Huxtable, was kind enough to write an appreciative note, a sentence of which expresses the aim of this little volume: " It has been a great help to me to read a book which has made the Easter episodes live." May the living Lord be pleased to use it to this end !

G.R.K.

West Croydon Tabernacle,
Eastertide, 1960.

BY WAY OF EXPLANATION

I SEND forth this little book with deep delight and with much misgiving. I face my readers with a very happy smile, but cast myself upon their mercy and understanding.

My delight is in the theme. The Easter story has a charm all its own. My heart has burned again while working over the manuscript. Perhaps Easter and The Forty Days to Ascensiontide are somewhat overshadowed by the pre-eminence of Calvary, and neglected a little in consequence. Books without number have been written upon the Cross and all the details of Good Friday's sequence of events, but comparatively few upon the closing six weeks of our Lord's earthly life. I have a feeling, too, that sometimes in the great works on the Life of Christ, the closing chapters are rather hurried, as though the writers were pressed for space or time or even patience towards the end. Not, of course, that this little volume is intended to remedy that defect in any way! If however it makes Easter and the days following a little more glowing for anyone, or flings out a suggestion or two to my brother preachers at Easter time (which is not the easiest season for pulpit preparation year after year) I shall be very glad indeed.

My misgiving is concerning the content and form of this book. Each chapter is a corrected shorthand record of Thursday evening studies given to my own congregation at what is called "The East London Bible School". They are the last seven of a five-year course on the earthly life of our Lord, and were delivered during the spring and summer of 1943. The course had to be interrupted during the winter months because of bombing, but in the lighter evenings we could all reach our homes before the raiders arrived. My faithful stenographer reproduced every word spoken, and I have found frequent reference to the bombings of those times and to casualties and disasters sustained. Preparation for these studies was made in the pressure of war-time in East London! And the delivery of these addresses was made extremely difficult by reason of our borrowed church for Thursday evenings being sideways on to the street and right flush with the pavement. In the East End the roadway is the children's only playground—and in the warm weather we had to have some windows open! To a preacher who feels he must have quietness at any cost, this was a hardship indeed. I find in the manuscript occasional pauses while a couple of stewards hurriedly leave the building to beg children to shout less or sing farther up the street, or have their roller-skate races in the next turning! Only the kindly attention and loyal support of that crowded hall kept me going at all, and made it possible to continue the series to the end. I mention this, not so much to excuse my many deficiencies herein displayed, but to explain to my indulgent readers that this volume is a product of the stress of war. Of course, the whole thing should have been rewritten—but that, in my present circumstances as a very pressed East London minister, is quite impossible. So, if my publisher is to have this book at all, it must be in this admittedly second best form: reported addresses as given, without material alteration.

My indebtedness is to an innumerable host of authors: as many of you will discern. I read widely and avidly for my Bible School work and, having a fairly retentive memory, am not always sure whether an idea is mine or someone else's. What have we, in any case, that we have not received? My beloved Principal, Dr. Percy Evans, used to say: " Cursed be all those who think our original thoughts before us! "

I hope I upset none of you. If I spoil a pet theory of yours, you will forbear with me. If I am obviously wrong, do me the great kindness of letting me know. If I handle a lovely thing with too rough fingers, or speak in a holy of holies with too loud a voice, I am extremely sorry. Let no one be put off by the first chapter. If you don't like it, go on to the next— and then return to the first, to give it careful attention.

Well, I cherish the hope that for some at least, as you turn over these awkward, ill-fashioned pages, the Easter Lord, in His great loving kindness, may speak again and hearts burn once more as He talks to you by the way.

G.R.K.

East London Tabernacle
1948

CHAPTER ONE

THE DIVINE MISSIONARY TO HADES

JESUS our Lord is dead on the Cross, His body cold and stiff. In this first study we follow His spirit into the unseen, beyond the gateway of death. On the Cross His final words were " ... into Thy hand I hand over My spirit " and two of the gospel writers in referring to the actual dying of the Saviour, put it this way: " He sent away His spirit." Whither did He send His spirit? Where in spirit did He go? Where are you going when your body becomes dead? Did Jesus go there? No, He did not. I am going straight to Heaven when I die, but Jesus did not go straight to Heaven when He died. After He had come back from the grave He said: " I am not yet ascended unto My Father." He did not then go to His Father—at least, we are not told that He did. Where did He go then? Well, we have some light from Scripture and that, of course, can be our only guide. What do we know for certain about the movements of Jesus in the spirit world beyond the earth?

One thing we know is that He went to Paradise and met the dying thief there. Then we know from Peter's pentecostal sermon, that Jesus went to Hades. Peter, quoting one of the Psalms, says, " Thou wilt not leave His soul in Hades". If God was not going to leave His soul in Hades, it follows logically that He went to Hades when He died. Those are two things we know for sure. There is a third thing we know by implication from Romans x. The Apostle says: " Who shall ascend into Heaven? [that is, to bring Christ down from above;] or, Who shall descend into the deep? [that is, to bring up Christ again from the dead]." So, when He was dead, He went into the deep; and that as you will see in the margin, means the abyss. The abyss is the domain of Satan and his angels, the bottomless pit, as it is called in Revelation.

So Jesus went into Paradise, the abode of the blessed dead; He went into Hades, the abode of all the dead, blessed and cursed, righteous and wicked; and He went into the abyss, the bottomless pit. That we are told in Scripture. Then Paul in Ephesians iv. tells us that He descended into the lower parts of the earth, whatever that means and wherever that is. Finally, in Peter's First Epistle and the third chapter we are told that after He had been put to death in the flesh but quickened in the spirit He went and preached to the spirits in prison, whoever they are and wherever they were. This then we are told with certainty from the Word of God. We must now sift these things out and try to understand exactly what they mean.

I

The Apostle Paul in Ephesians iv. speaks of the gifts made by Christ to the Church and at the eighth verse he quotes from Psalm lxviii., Ephesians iv. 8. " Wherefore He saith "—now this is the Psalm—" When He ascended up on high, He led captivity captive and gave gifts unto men." And then something in brackets, intensely interesting. (" Now that He ascended, what is it but that He also descended first into the lower parts of the earth? He that descended is the same also that ascended up far above all heavens, that He might fill all things "). Now, I warn you at once that we are travelling on difficult ground. Nothing that I shall say shall I speak dogmatically: I only give you, after very careful study, my own interpretation of this part of our Saviour's pilgrimage. Others of you may have other interpretations and I shall not quarrel with you and you must not quarrel with me, but I must tell you what I believe to be the truth about these matters.

It is rather unfortunate that the great Apostles' Creed has misled us all these years. What is the wording of that noble declaration of faith? " He suffered under Pontius Pilate, was crucified, dead and buried, He descended into hell; the third day He rose again from the dead." " He descended into hell." Now in the day of the Apostles' Creed and later on in the day

when the Authorised Version was translated for us (1611),
" Hell " did not have the dread associations that it has now.
Hell simply means a covered-in place. In the old English
game of forefeits, " the hell " was the covered-in place where
the girl, screaming with laughter, hid to escape from the
kisses, or I suppose, in some cases, did *not* try to escape from
them! They called it a " hell ", a covered-in place. To this
day in Devonshire a thatcher who covers-in is called a
" hellier ". So that is the meaning of hell. In the Authorised
Version the word " hell " was used to translate two Greek
words: " Hades " and " Gehenna ". Now it is very unfortunate that in our English Bible " hell " should be used for
two entirely different states, and this has led to misunder-
standing.

So let us get our terms right at once. In the Old Testament
the word is " Sheol ". Sometimes it is rendered " the grave ",
sometimes " hell ", but it is always the Hebrew word
" Sheol ". " Thou wilt not leave My soul in Sheol,"—the
same word which Peter quoted on the day of Pentecost. In
the New Testament the word is " Hades ", and the Revisers
have put " Hades " in place of " hell " whenever it should be
thus rendered. Now " Sheol " in the Old Testament and
" Hades " in the New Testament are exactly equivalent.
They refer to the same place and state and they both mean
" the unseen ", that is to say, " the great beyond " after this
life is passed.

Now the Jews in the Old Testament, and in the New, had
a very kindergarten idea of astronomy; they did not know
then that the earth was round and there was no reason why
God should have revealed it to them—though, incidentally, in
Scripture there are indications that the earth is a globe—the
Bible is never contrary to science, remember. But the Jews
did not understand that the earth was round, a globe; they
thought of it as a great flat plain, floating through space as a
broad leaf floats through the air. And the upper part of the
leaf, if you like, was lit by the sun and inhabited by the living,
our world; the underside of the leaf was dark, unlit by the sun,
gloomy, and was the abode of the dead. So that, to the very

simple thinking of the early people of the Bible, you are on the upper part of the leaf when you are alive and when you die you go underneath. So every reference to Sheol in the Old Testament is down, and we have such expressions as "Sheol beneath". It is always subterranean, under the earth. The underworld, you see. Amos said: "If thou dig into Sheol"—always that idea of going underneath the earth to the under-side. Sometimes it is translated "the nether part of the earth". So Paul in Ephesians iv. says: "He descended into the lower parts of the earth," thus keeping to the old conventional idea of the underworld. The Bible tells us, then —I am using the past tense always because after Calvary things were different—the Bible tells us that Hades or Sheol was the afterworld of the dead, both blessed and cursed, both righteous and wicked.

Then the Bible tells us a further thing about the underworld. It is divided into two compartments. The Saviour refers to them both in the parable of Dives and Lazarus. The one compartment is Paradise, the other, Gehenna. Paradise is the abode of the righteous; Gehenna is the abode of the wicked. Paradise, in the Saviour's parable, is referred to as "Abraham's bosom", a lovely designation by the pious Jews. Gehenna is referred to as the place of torment. And between the two, you remember, is a great gulf fixed. Over that gulf there is no bridge. Neither from Paradise into Gehenna can they pass over, nor from Gehenna into Paradise. So in the Old Testament and in the Gospels everyone who died went into Hades or Sheol. Those who believed in God and obeyed Him, the righteous, were amongst the blessed in Paradise or Abraham's bosom; those who disbelieved in God and refused to obey Him went into the place of torment, the abode of the wicked.

The warden of Hades was Satan. In that marvellous second chapter of Hebrews, speaking of Christ's conquest when He died, the writer refers to "him that had the power of death, that is, the devil". The word means "the government"— him who was the governor of death, the devil. So, in the Old Testament and in the Gospels, everyone who died went into the wardenship of Satan, some into blessing, others into cursing, but all alike into Satan's keeping. Satan had the keys of the door of the grave.

II

And what happened when Jesus died?
"For He invaded death's abode
And robb'd him of his sting.
The house of dust enthralls no more,
For He, the strong to save,
Himself doth guard that silent door,
Great Keeper of the grave."

Jesus did something once and for all to the underworld when He left His dead body on the Cross. What He did has been perfectly expressed in the great Golden Legend, that wonderful medieval poetry which is often so true to Scripture.

"One day, in Satan's realm—the dark domain,
Where souls of dead in chains of death remain,
The Prince of darkness, boastful, spake aloud
To his abject, imprisoned, awestruck crowd:
'Hearken, ye spirits. Lo, I bring this day
Another victim bound beneath my sway:
Jesus, the Nazarene, the Master Fraud—
Who proudly claims Himself the Son of God!
I laid the snare, which the Impostor caught,
And to the tree of shame the Boaster brought;
And now, between two thieves He helpless hangs,
In Death's dissolving and resistless pangs.
You shall behold Him pass through Hades' door,
To walk among the living—nevermore!
My power shall hush the Archpretender's breath,
And bind Him hopeless in the realms of death.'

" Then Hell itself in fear began to quake,
And, in alarm, thus to the Devil spake,
' Jesus! Dost thou not fear that mighty Name?
And is this Jesus—Nazarene—the same
Who once cried, " Lazarus! Come forth! " and swift
The bands of death were loosed, his fetters rift,
And through thy gates impassable he broke,
So soon as that almighty word was spoke?
Let but that Jesus once invade these halls,
And in that hour thy boasted empire falls!
What if the victim thou dost proudly claim
Shall as the Victor bring thy pride to shame? '

" While Hell thus spake, a voice like thunder rolls
Throughout the realm of Death's imprisoned souls:
' Lift up your heads, ye everlasting gates!
The King of Glory at your entrance waits.'
Then Hell inquires, ' Who is this glorious King? '
And with the answer all its chambers ring:
' The Lord of Hosts—strong to subdue all foes,
Mighty in battle—none can Him oppose.'

" Then, in the realm of Death's unbroken shade
Appeared the Conqueror in light arrayed.
It was as tho' in crimson and in gold
The splendour of a thousand suns had rolled
Their mingled glory in one matchless beam,
And lit up Death Shade with the lustrous gleam.
Ineffable that glory; as it shone
Like to the radiance of the Great White Throne,
Precipitate, demons of darkness fled,
And lost souls, to the confines of the dead.
Whilst through the open gates and broken bars,
Toward realms of light more fadeless than the stars,
The Prince of Life a host of captives led
From out the night and bondage of the dead."

That's grand, isn't it? And so far as Scripture indicates, that is true. He went into these lower parts of the earth, this underworld, and He led captivity captive when He ascended on high. That is presumably what took place. The Saviour went into the world of the dead, conquered the warden and master of that place, wrenched from his grasp the keys of death and of Hades, so that ever since Good Friday night Christ has held the keys. He says so in Revelation i., you remember: " I am He that liveth; I became dead, and behold, I am alive for evermore; and I have the keys of death and of Hades." Satan had them before: I have them now. Then when Jesus ascended He took these released captives under Satan's government with Him up into Heaven. That is why I have called this study " The Divine Missionary to Hades".

Now think what this means. It means that the moment Jesus died on earth to accomplish the redemption of a lost world, He went to visit all the old friends of His Father (and His friends, too) in the Old Testament, from righteous Abel right on to the last believer in God who had died before Calvary. You see, they were all there—all the Old Testament saints, all the patriarchs, the godly women, the believers in God, great and small, old and young—they were all there. Many of them had seen, in sacrifice and ceremony, the symbol of our salvation accomplished on Calvary. They had looked forward to what it was going to mean. Now they meet the Saviour Himself, the fulfilment of all the ritual of the Old Testament. " They hailed His coming from afar ", and now they pay their homage at His feet. How glad they must have been to see Him! Two of them had seen Him before, Moses and Elijah, but they were the only privileged two.

So I follow Him in imagination down in the vaults of the dead, into Paradise where the blessed dead were and I see them bow at His feet and He tells them all that has been accomplished at Calvary, and all that is going to mean and He gives them the opportunity of accepting the gospel. There is a verse in 1 Peter iv. 6 which speaks of the gospel being preached to the dead. I cannot tell you whether it refers to this. It is an obscure passage, but I mention it here for its interest. " For this cause was the gospel preached also to them that are dead, that they might be judged according to men in the flesh, but live according to God in the spirit." I wonder if that means that Jesus gave the saints of the Old Testament a chance of accepting the gospel, and, that those who did believe Him He took with Him to Heaven when He ascended. Now that is a fact that we know, that He took them with Him into Heaven, and ever since Ascension Day Paradise has changed its place. Before the day of Ascension, Paradise was in Hades, and it was one part of the afterworld, a great gulf's breadth away from Gehenna, the place of torment. But when Jesus ascended into Heaven from Olivet, He took with Him Paradise, transferred Paradise into Heaven where it is now. And all who believe the gospel when He preached it as a Divine Missionary to Hades went up to Heaven with Him and are there now, and our dear dead who die in the Lord are there with them. If you were to die tonight and you are a Christian, you would join their blissful company immediately.

In Ephesians i, in the verse describing Christ's resurrection from the dead, the Holy Spirit puts together the biggest words for strength in the Greek language; and it is undoubtedly true, that the greatest output of energy mentioned in the Bible was the energy God needed to expend to lift Jesus from the tomb to the Throne, because Scripture says all the hosts of darkness were against the resurrection from the tomb to the Throne. Well, now you can understand it.

" . . . He hath crushed beneath His rod
The World's proud rebel king.
He plunged in His imperial strength
To gulfs of darkness down;
He brought His trophy up at length,
The foiled usurper's crown."

And so, from the tomb on Easter morning to the Throne on Ascension Day, the devil was madly contesting Christ's right, but God, of course, won, and ever since that time Satan has been bereft of the keys of the afterworld for all who die believing in Christ. Well, that is one thing Jesus did when He died. So now, living this side of the Cross, as I say, we go straight to Heaven.

It does not come in the purview of our study to consider Immortality. That is a stage further on, another privilege, the higher Heaven which Christ brings us into at the Second Advent. The New Jerusalem at the end of Revelation is a higher stage still beyond that, the ultimate dwelling place of the redeemed. So our dear dead in Christ, though they are in Heaven and are with Christ, have not yet experienced the full glory of the Beyond. They are going to do that with us when Jesus comes again, " that they without us should not be made perfect," as Hebrews xi says. When we die now we go to " the spirits of just men made perfect ". Their spirits were made perfect on the day of Ascension, when they were delivered from the bondage of death under Satan's governorship to Heaven with Christ, but that is only their *spirit* which has been perfected. At his return He is going to come with a glorified body and then their whole personality, body and spirit, will be made perfect with our own. But that is another story! That is Immortality, a privilege yet to come.

Before I pass on to the next stage of what Jesus did, let us read that passage in Hebrews ii, so that we can be quite clear on the Scriptural evidence of this. Hebrews ii. 14. " Forasmuch then as the children are partakers of flesh and blood, He also Himself likewise took part of the same; "—now look!—" that through death He might bring to naught " —render inoperative—" him that had the government of death, that is, the devil; and deliver "—you see?—" deliver them who through fear of death were all their lifetime subject to bondage." The deliverance was from Hades to Heaven, the first stage of which Jesus accomplished on Good Friday night, the second stage of which He accomplished on the day of Ascension. But that is not all He did while His body hung on the Cross and was later buried in a tomb.

III

There is yet another passage which must be considered—
I Peter iii. 19—but first read the eighteenth verse, and here
we are on a still fiercer battlefield of the commentators. " For
Christ also hath once suffered for sins, the just for the unjust,
that He might bring us to God, being put to death in the flesh
but made alive in spirit." Now the Authorised Version is not
correct there when it says, " by the Spirit " with a capital " S ".
This is not the Holy Spirit. It means that, when His flesh
died, His spirit was living: and (v. 19, in the living spirit,
which He commended to His Father and then sent away, in
that spirit also He went and preached unto the spirits in
prison. Well now, who are these folk? Are they not the
same beings as those we have been considering? These
people are called captives who were under the governorship
of Satan in Hades; will not these spirits in prison fit in there
nicely with what I have said before? I am afraid not, because—
read on " . . . spirits in prison, which sometime were dis-
obedient, when once the longsuffering of God waited in the
days of Noah. . . ." These are not the general dead of the Old
Testament saints, then: these have to do with just the days
of Noah—" while the ark was a preparing, wherein few, that
is, eight souls were saved by water " and so on. So these
spirits in prison have to do with the Flood.

It would take a long time to explain to you the why's and
the wherefore's of the interpretation I am going to give here,
but I will tell you who these spirits in prison seem undoubtedly
to be. They are the fallen angels of Genesis vi. In Genesis vi
we are told that the Devil, to destroy the seed-of-the-woman
line from which the Messiah was coming, tried to corrupt the
whole human race. He did it by making the sons of God
(always referring to angels) marry the daughters of men and
they brought forth a race of giants. Satan had the power to
take his fallen angels who had been cast out of Heaven and
to bring them on to the earth in bodily form; and these in-
carnate demons married human women and produced a race
of demonised mankind, so wicked that the whole earth became

utterly corrupt. Indeed, every family on earth was guilty of this demon-marriage save one family, the family of Noah. One family only refused to inter-marry with these demon giants. That is why Noah's family was saved in the ark. The world became so diabolically wicked under these demonised men that the only thing God could do was to destroy the race, which He did with the Flood. When the demonised people perished in the waters of the Flood their spirits immediately went into the abode of the cursed, Gehenna, only, being angels, they went deeper than Gehenna. Now, turn the pages of your New Testament and you will find where they went. 2 Peter ii. 4. Here you see light upon the situation. You will notice that in verse 5 Peter is talking about Noah again; we are still in the same context. " For if God spared not the angels which sinned but cast them down to hell "—but the Greek word is " tartarus "—" and delivered them into chains of darkness "—these are the spirits *in prison*—" *chains* of darkness to be reserved unto judgment." Then if you want further facts about them, turn over to Jude and you will find that in the sixth verse of his epistle he throws still more light upon these demon angels. Jude 6. " And the angels which kept not their first estate "—which was that of being angels; they became angel-men—" but left their own habitation "—they came on to this earth and made their home here with the daughters of men, you see—" He hath reserved in everlasting chains under darkness unto the judgment of the great day." So you see, if you agree with this interpretation, the spirits in prison are those people in Noah's day, who had the long-suffering of God for over a hundred years while the ark was being built—a century of opportunity for repentance—and these are the people to whom the Saviour went between Good Friday evening and Easter Sunday morning.

So first He went into Hades, the underworld; then He went lower, into the abyss, the bottomless pit, Tartarus, the abode of the Devil and his angels. In this connection it is interesting to find that a difficult passage of Paul becomes clearer with this in mind. 1 Timothy iii. 16. " And without controversy great is the mystery of godliness: God was manifest in the flesh, justified in the Spirit, seen of angels, preached unto the Gentiles, believed on in the world, received up into glory." One other question which is possibly upon your mind is: when He preached unto the spirits in prison, did He give those fallen angels a chance to repent? I think not. The word translated " preach " is not the word " to evangelise ", which is the word for preaching the gospel; it is the word " to herald ", " to proclaim ". No, I think the Saviour went down into the bottomless pit and showed Himself as the Conqueror of their proud master, to tell them of what He had done, and set His seal to their doom.

IV

Finally, go back to Ephesians iv. At the end of this paragraph in brackets: verse 10. " He that descended is the same also that ascended up far above all heavens, that He might fill all things." There is our glorious Lord, the Conqueror with the nail-pierced hands! He went to the lowest depths of hell, the bottomless pit; He ascended to the highest heights of Heaven, the Throne of God. He has passed through the heavens and He is at the height of Heaven, the Throne of God; and the Spirit through Paul in this verse says He did that in order that He might fill all things. In other words, from the lowest depths of hell, the abode of Satan, to the highest height of Heaven, the abode of God, Christ is Conqueror. On earth, on Good Friday afternoon, I see a white corpse, having been bleeding on a Cross, the very picture of human weakness. He is dead! But that is not Jesus Christ: that is only His earthly body. To see Christ in that moment you need to put all His glorious apparel on; you need to clothe Him in all His majesty; for He is invading a universe, filling all things! By virtue of His dying as this world's Redeemer, He is supreme in Heaven—He fills the Throne! He is supreme on earth: none can stay His hand. He is supreme in the world of the dead, even down to the depths of hell where the devil's angels are held captive for the last great Assize. The Mighty Lord! Mightiest in Heaven! Mightiest on earth! Mightiest in hell! Lord of the universe! Lord of eternity! Best of all, my own dear Saviour! And when my last breath has left my body, I am going straight There to Him, to " the glorious land He has gone to prepare for all who are washed and forgiven". Are *you* going there when you die? It depends on whether you obey and trust this Mighty Saviour in your present life, while there is time.

CHAPTER TWO

EASTER MORNING

Reading: John xx. 1–18

As soon as we come to consider the events of Easter Day, we are amidst romance and problems. There is no more thrilling page in Scripture than the page which tells of Easter morning—and there is no more difficult page! For, you see, the four gospel writers all record the rising of Christ from the dead—at least, that needs qualifying at once, for none of them, strikingly enough, records the actual resurrection of Jesus. No man saw Him actually rise from the dead nor come forth from the grave. So, just as there are no details given of the crucifying of Jesus, so there are no details given of His rising, but all four writers do present us with the fact, showing the effects of the fact and the proofs of the fact. Well now, that seems to present no difficulty until we begin to read the four records together. Read any one of them by itself and there is no difficulty, but read all four of them one after the other and immediately you see that there is a very real problem to fit them all in with one another.

Let us briefly run through the facts as set out in Matthew, Mark, Luke and John. I am simply reminding you of what you are already familiar with. Matthew tells us that Mary Magdalene and the other Mary, who turns out to be Mary the Mother of James and Joses, have come to see the sepulchre; there is an earthquake; the angel of the Lord descends, rolls back the stone, and the keepers, the watch set to guard the tomb, are rendered as good as dead. The angel immediately turns to the two women and says, emphatically, " Fear not *ye*, for I know what you have come for. He is not here; go, tell His disciples." " And they did run to bring His disciples word." And as they were going the Saviour Himself met them. That is Matthew's account. Mary Magdalene and the other Mary—just two of them.

Now when we turn to Mark we find that there are three women mentioned, Mary Magdalene, Mary the Mother of James (presumably the " other Mary ") and Salome, the Mother of James and John, the wife of Zebedee. They are going to the sepulchre—so Mark tells us: they wonder who is going to roll away the stone, and when they reach it they find it is rolled away and they see a young man sitting on the right side clothed in a long white garment. He speaks to them to the same effect as to Matthew's two Marys, but by no means in the same words. He says: " Tell Peter as well as the disciples." Then we are told that these three women were so frightened that they never said a word to anybody, whereas Matthew's two Marys run quickly to bring the disciples word.

How does Luke tell the story of Easter morning? Luke says there were quite a number of the women who came to the sepulchre; Mary Magdalene and Joanna and Mary the Mother of James—the two Marys again—but this time Joanna is mentioned and other women that were with them. Now Luke's company of women are met by *two* angels at the sepulchre and the two angels in Luke's account quote Scripture, quote what the Saviour has said: " The Son of Man must be delivered into the hands of sinful men and be crucified and the third day rise again." A quite different story, you see. But Luke's women go and tell the apostles.

Now when we come to John we find that John, as often, writing so long after the other three, supplements entirely new information, and John's record tells how Mary came alone, was distracted to find the stone moved away, ran to tell Peter and John, they in turn ran to the sepulchre, leaving Mary behind, and Mary is met by the Saviour Himself, and then she goes and tells the disciples.

Well, that may not appear to you at once to present such insuperable difficulties, but if you come to think about it you will find that it is very difficult indeed. The great problem is to reconcile Matthew and John. If I were to ask all of you individually the first thing that happened on Easter morning you would say: " Oh well, the angel of the Lord came down and rolled back the stone from the door of the sepulchre— that is how it all began." But wait just a moment. Supposing that is so, then unless I entirely misread Matthew's account, Mary and the other Mary were there at that moment, and whereas the watchers were as dead men, the angel said to the women: " Fear not ye . . . " and in the Greek the " ye " is emphatic, clearly pointing to the fact that the angel is saying: " Now the keepers are frightened to death, but don't you be afraid because you seek Jesus—you are His friends." Now if that is the first thing that happens on Easter morning and if subsequently Mary and the other Mary run to tell the disciples and are met by Jesus Himself, then why does Mary Magdalene suddenly change her whole mood and cry her eyes out at the sepulchre because they have taken away the Lord and nobody knows where He is? It is illogical, isn't it? So what are we to do? Either Matthew is right or John is right. But when we come to Mark we are met with another problem. Mark tells us that Jesus " appeared first to Mary Magdalene ", so we must put John first. Oh, but then that won't do, because John tells us that the stone was rolled away when Mary arrived at the sepulchre. But Mary was there all the time. What can you do with it? It is hopeless!

Well, you can, if you will, deal with it as the infidels and the higher critics deal with it. You can talk about " the ten discrepancies ". Those whose delight is to discredit the gospels and the inspiration of Scripture have a right royal gala time with these four accounts of Easter morning. They don't deny the resurrection but they do say: " Well now, look at your record! Here is the most important thing upon which Christianity rests and you have the four gospel writers denying one another in the records." Obviously, that won't do for you and it won't do for me. The explanation is not that the records are unreliable. Well, if you won't have that explanation you can have another, which I would say is the commonly accepted explanation amongst Bible students. That is that here you have the records as told by very excited people on

Easter morning, and therefore you cannot expect to have *exact* details of what took place. People were taken by surprise: they were thrilled, frightened, delighted in turn: and excited as they were, and therefore not in a position to give a detailed and accurate record, they all make some gift to the whole picture, and you have just to take the four accounts and try and make one picture of them all, and remember that it is what very excited people said. That, I say at once, is not good enough for me. And I trust it is not good enough for you. You will find that in effect in most of the commentaries. But, I find that the Holy Spirit, the Editor of the sacred Scriptures, is always meticulously careful in details. I find nothing of this excitability in any other part of the records, and I am not prepared to find it here. No, no, my own spirit refuses to be satisfied until I can find that these four apparently contradictory records are actually supplementary and all are true and fill in an accurate picture.

It takes some doing to get to that position, I assure you. I must confess that I have put away all my books, not being able to find complete satisfaction in any of them, and I have spent hours just with my Bible and my Greek Testament to see exactly what was written. And I believe I have a satisfying picture to show you: at any rate my own heart and mind are completely satisfied.

Let me point out one obvious fact, before we look at the records themselves: Mary Magdalene held a position among the women friends of Jesus corresponding to the position Simon Peter held amongst the men. Mary is the unofficial but acknowledged leader of the women. Throughout the whole of this crisis during the week-end of Good Friday and Easter, that is so. Interestingly enough, therefore, we find that the Saviour first reveals Himself to Mary alone and then reveals Himself to Simon Peter alone. " The Lord hath appeared unto Simon ", you remember, only we are not told anything about *that* interview. Again, interestingly enough, Mary Magdalene is invariably mentioned first among the list of women, as Simon Peter is mentioned first amongst the list of men. Then we find on Easter morning that Mary has a dear faithful lieutenant of the same name. Now I am going to throw out the suggestion to you, verifying it as I go through, that on Easter morning Mary Magdalene went round to all the women followers of Jesus, accompanied often by this other Mary, and they, as it were, whipped up the other women to go to the sepulchre. At this point let me just quote a verse of Elizabeth Barrett Browning on Mary Magdalene.

> " Not she, with traitorous kiss, her Master stung:
> Not she denied Him with unfaithful tongue:
> She, when disciples fled, could dangers brave:
> Last at the cross, and earliest at the grave."

Let that poetic tribute be laid at the feet of this noble woman.

When I came to study my Greek Testament I found the clue: I found that each of the four gospel writers, Matthew, Mark, Luke and John, as though prompted by one over-ruling Editor, in the opening sentences of their accounts are very careful to state the time at which the things they are going to tell took place. I am going to begin with John because he begins earliest in time. John says: " When it was yet dark "; that is to say, before Easter day has come: there was the light of the full moon, but it was yet dark. It is night when John records. Matthew begins: " As it began to dawn towards the first day of the week ". As it *began* to dawn. The first faint flush of the new day is appearing in the sky—that is Matthew. Luke says, in the Authorised Version: " Very early in the morning "; but literally " at deep dawn ". I find from contemporary writings that the Greek meant by that " Dawn well broken ",—not as day began to dawn but with the dawn over-spreading the sky: dawn complete. Mark uses the same words in the Authorised Version: " Very early in the morning ", but it is not at deep dawn: it is just the ordinary way of saying " Very early in the morning ". Then Mark adds this: " at the rising of the sun ", which in the Revised Version is more correctly translated " when the sun was risen ".

You see very clearly that these four times are quite different and they are all put foremost in the narrative as though they were important. Now they would not be important in the ordinary way. It doesn't matter a bit whether it is still night or whether it is just beginning to dawn or whether the dawn is finished or whether the sun is up, as to the events of the morning. So it rather looks as though there is some special point in so clearly and carefully marking the times in their various records. Just as clearly, John comes first, " When it was yet dark ". Matthew comes next, " As the day began to dawn ". Luke comes third, " At deep dawn ". And Mark comes fourth, "When the sun was risen". Have a care to remember that in the East the coming of dawn is very much quicker than here in the West. It is impossible for me not to remember the dawn that I saw from Mount Niesen in Switzerland. What an experience! But in the East all this would take place in perhaps an hour or less, from night to the sun beginning to rise, but quite long enough for what I am going to tell you about to take place.

With this clue I think I can safely proceed along that line. So what happened first? John tells us. " When it was yet dark." Now let us turn to our Bibles. John xx first of all. " The first day of the week cometh Mary Magdalene early when it was yet dark, unto the sepulchre, and seeth the stone taken away from the sepulchre." Here again one is rewarded by the careful notice of the words the Holy Spirit used. Matthew, Mark and Luke, in the burial of the Saviour and in the resurrection of the Saviour, referred to the stone being rolled. You are all familiar with the Eastern tomb where the round disc is placed against the door and can be rolled along a groove, leaving the entrance of the tomb clear. John, however, does not use the time-honoured expression which had already been written in these three previous gospels: he uses " taken away ", and literally " lifted out of " the sepulchre. Therefore, you see, when it was yet dark, when Mary came alone at night, the stone had not been rolled away—that follows later—it had been lifted out of the sepulchre. Don't ask me where it was! I can't tell you—it just wasn't there.

They had watched, these women, they had watched the Roman soldiers seal that stone after it had been rolled into its place; now when Mary at night, in the light of the moon, comes to the sepulchre she sees to her horror that the stone is nowhere to be seen, lifted right out of the sepulchre.

Mary's one horror was that somebody would get into that tomb and take away the body of the Lord. I say that, because it was Mary who stayed the whole night of Good Friday mounting self-imposed vigil over the tomb. She only went away from the tomb during the hours of the Sabbath. I am glad to find that Mary kept her Sabbath observation faithfully, even though she would love to have lingered at the grave, never to take her eyes off it. That is a challenge for some of you Sabbath-breakers of to-day! And without going to investigate very closely, seeing the stone taken away, she comes to the worst possible conclusion and rushes back breathless to Peter and John. " They have taken away the Lord out of the sepulchre and we know not where they have laid Him." " *We* know not. . . ." So on the way back she had just gone to the other Mary and had broken the awful news and then dashed off to Peter and John. Like a woman, that—not stopping to investigate, but going by her own impulse and instinct and intuition, not waiting for proof! Ah, and it is interesting to find where Peter was during Good Friday and black Sabbath. I am glad John took Peter home with him. I wonder, if John had not found Simon Peter and taken him to his own home, whether we might not have had two suicides instead of one. But under the influence of John and the Lord's mother, Peter was at any rate kept sane and safe.

The two disciples arise at once and run to the sepulchre. John gets there first. Does that mean that John was the younger man? He had more breath—he didn't talk as much as Peter did! Anyway, he got there first and stooped down and looked in and saw the linen clothes lying but, with reticence, went not in. Then up comes Peter—Peter, as we should expect, with no reticence at all, goes blindly in straightway, and Peter sees the linen clothes and the napkin. Then John went in also and he saw and believed. Now what did they see? They saw the winding shrouds exactly and precisely as they were when He was buried. I have done much reading for this study to know what other people think about it and have read pages of rubbish about Jesus always being neat and orderly, and when He had risen from the dead, unwinding the shrouds from His own living body, and very carefully putting this here and that there and the napkin in a nice neat little pile just apart. What nonsense! Why didn't these men read their Greek testaments? That was not what Peter and John saw at all. They simply saw the winding sheets as they had been, with this difference, that the body was not there. They were empty. Nothing had happened to the shrouds at all. They had not been touched. They were simply there but without the body. John saw that *and believed*. Mary was the first to *see* Jesus alive, but John was the first to *know* that He was alive.

The different words for " seeing " here are very interesting in the Greek, very illuminating. " Seeing them ": at first Mary and John merely saw the facts: then Peter went in and he " beheld them " (R.V.) which means he saw and he thought carefully about them. Then John *saw*, perceived what it meant (a different word: a word which means to " see with understanding "), he perceived what it meant *and believed*, and from that moment John was convinced that Jesus was alive. The others did not yet realise that He was alive, but John did. You might have asked just now: " Why didn't Jesus show Himself first to His particular friend? " Well, for this reason: John did not need that manifestation. Of John it could have been said then that he was amongst those blessed ones who saw not and yet believed.

Now they go back home, John understanding, Peter all bewildered; and they leave Mary at the tomb. Presumably Mary was not with them when they were making their inspection, but she is lingering around in the garden somewhere, and when they have gone, she is standing at the sepulchre weeping—not just crying, but convulsed with sobs. There are two angels in the tomb now and they ask her why she weeps and she says a lovely thing: " Because they have taken

away *my lord. . . .*" He is dead: His body has been rifled from
the tomb: it is all over: but He is still " *MY LORD* "—that
is a lovely touch. Splendid-hearted Mary! " They have taken
away my Lord and I know not where they have laid Him."
Then without waiting for an answer from the angels, for she
is inconsolable in her grief, she turns herself back and there is
a figure in the dim light of the moon. Through her tears she
does not know who it is, and thinks it must be the gardener.

He says to her, " Why weepest thou? Whom seekest
thou? " " Sir, if thou hast borne Him hence tell me where thou
hast laid Him and I will take Him away." Of course, she could
not have carried the full-grown body of a splendidly built
man, but then again, the love of a noble woman never stops to
be reasonable. Nor does she pause to consider what the gardener would be doing there at night. "I will take Him away,"
she says, not realising that she could not have done that even
if it had been given her to do so. Then suddenly, that voice!
Her name! No one will ever know how He said " Mary ".
But she is at His feet. " My Master." It must have been worth
dying and being buried to Jesus just to have that from Mary,
I think, and to see the transformation in that splendid woman.

" Touch Me not," He says. Now that is misleading, you
know, in the Authorised Version—not incorrect, but misleading. The Revisers in the margin have given the more
accurate rendering: " Take not hold of Me. . . ." It does not
mean that He forbade Mary to touch Him. In the upper room
that evening He said to the disciples: " Come and touch Me,
see that I am real." You see, she was clinging hold to Him
as though she would never let Him go. And He says, " Mary,
don't take hold of Me like that, for I am not yet ascended to
My Father. Mary, it is different now; the old order changeth
yielding place to new. Mary, I am going back to God and
then I am going to send you the Spirit and you are going to
take hold of Him in a more real way still. Don't cling to Me—
you mustn't now—it is different now—it is going to be
different. Take not hold of Me, but go and tell My brethren.
. . ." And she went and told them. Now it is still night.
Easter Day has not yet dawned. But He rose the third day!

Ah! but you will find that in " the third day " and " the third night " and so on, the Scriptural idiom is very loose to our way of thinking and they used " night " and " morning " indiscriminately; it does not make any difference to the truth of the Word that as yet it is not officially the new day; it is still night.

We must go now to Matthew. Matthew xxviii. 1. " As it began to dawn towards the first day of the week." Mary, having told Peter and John that she has seen the Lord and having told them what He has said to her (John xx. 18), now thinks of her faithful lieutenant, the other Mary; and she and the other Mary go to the sepulchre. The day is by this time beginning to dawn. " . . . as it began to dawn." While they are on their way to the sepulchre, behold, an earthquake, and the angel of the Lord—not just *an* angel, but *the* angel of the Lord—descended from heaven and came and rolled back the stone from the door and sat upon it. That, I suggest, is the ceremonial opening of the tomb. Not, of course, to let the Lord out—He is out already; He was out before the stone was ever moved—but to show the fact to everyone, foe and friend alike, that the tomb is empty. Suggestively enough, this ceremonial opening by the special angel happens at the moment of dawn. The new day begins and the angel comes to earth as we have seen, the keepers are as dead men, and the angel says to the women: " Fear not *ye* "; and going down the verses to v. 7, the angel adds: " and go quickly and tell His disciples that He is risen from the dead, and behold "— and this is a new message now—" He goeth before you into Galilee: there shall ye see Him. Lo, I have told you." And they departed quickly from the sepulchre with fear and with great joy and did run to bring His disciples word, and as they went to tell . . . Jesus met them.

What happens next? Turn to Luke. He continues the narrative. Luke xxiv. 1. And this, remember, is at deep dawn. By now the light of the dawn, the flaming pageantry of the new day, is spreading all across the sky. Dawn is well broken. Here is another party coming to the sepulchre: Mary Magdalene and the other Mary and, with them in this party, Joanna and other women. They are coming to the sepulchre a little later, and they are all bringing the spices which they had prepared with loving care. Perhaps the two Marys had not seen the extravagant embalming operations of Joseph and Nicodemus, or perhaps they felt that they too must have a share in this last tender office. They find the stone rolled away; they enter in; find not the body of the Lord Jesus; then v. 4 " . . . it came to pass as they were much perplexed thereabout . . ."—you see, the two Marys are not with them at this stage; they have told them to go to the sepulchre and have joined them later, but they are not with them now obviously or there would be no perplexity—" . . . behold, two men . . . in shining garments "—a second angel now. And the two angels together speak to this party of women slightly differently. " Why seek ye the living among the dead? He is not here, but is risen; remember how He spake unto you when He was yet in Galilee, saying . . ." And they quote the Lord's own words. The women remember and they go back and tell, having been joined on the way by the two Marys; and the disciples didn't believe them. Cleopas says, you remember: " Certain women came and they said . . . but, you know what women are! They didn't convince us." Ah, but look, v. 12. " Then arose Peter and ran to the sepulchre." So Peter's off again. Yes, Peter's off again. Peter could not sit still! Peter cannot understand it yet, and he goes and sees the same things and comes away still unbelieving, wondering in himself at that which was come to pass. So twice Peter went to the tomb. It would be impossible for Peter to keep still for three seconds running! I marvel that he only went twice! He may have gone more than twice but we are told of two occasions when he ran to the tomb. Poor Peter! He has not seen Jesus yet, and his heart is in an earthquake!

Well, is that all? No! No! Mark continues the narrative. " When the sun was risen." Ah, now dawn is a thing of the past and the sun has risen and Mark presents us with still another group of womenfolk, amongst whom is Salome. And here are the two Marys again; they are behind it; they are dodging about as I suspect from one group of women to

another, as breathless as Peter, telling all the women: " Go
to the sepulchre! Don't ask us to tell you what has happened,
but go to the sepulchre." Here then is another party going.
It is daylight now; the sun is beginning to rise; they ask about
the stone—you see, they have not properly heard yet—they
find the stone rolled away; and when they get there there is
only one angel, and to them he appeared as a young man.
Angels are eternally young. The dew of their youth is upon
them. " Age shall not weary them nor the years condemn."
A young man in shining raiment, he is called. They were
very frightened, and he says: " Be not affrighted; ye seek
Jesus of Nazareth which was crucified: He is risen; He is not
here: behold the place where they laid Him. But go your way,
tell His disciples *and Peter.* . . ." It is this angel to these women
who says: " Don't forget Peter. Peter keeps coming to the
tomb and going away again; tell Peter." I wonder that the
angel did not speak to Peter himself, but he must have had
good reason for not doing so. Perhaps the Lord had told
him: " Leave Peter to Me. I'll deal with him personally."
But the angel says to these women: " Now be sure you tell
Peter." The sad thing is that they were too frightened to tell
anybody. " Neither said they anything to any man, for they
were afraid." My dear friends, has God given you a very
special message for some particular person at some particular
time of need and you have been too frightened to say anything? What a pity for poor Peter that they did not tell him
what they were bidden!

Now do you agree? Does that seem to you to make sense?
Does it make a new Easter morning story for you? The more
I think about it the more satisfied I am with it, though I have
no one else in the world to confirm it for me.

There is just one thing more. It is not only the *friends* of
Jesus who are busy; and frightened; and running about on
Easter morning. For if you turn, in closing, back to Matthew,
you will find from v. 11 to 15 a rather sorry tale. " Now when
they were going . . ." that is, the women, " to tell the disciples "—and this, of course, is still at the beginning of dawn,
for the two referred to are the two Marys—" behold some of

the watch came into the city and showed unto the chief priests all the things which were done." The watchmen have recovered now. " And when they were assembled with the elders," that is, the chief priests—which indicates another hurriedly-called meeting of the Sanhedrin. Poor Caiaphas, he cannot get a decent night's rest! He has to whip up the Sanhedrin, for something terrible has happened. " And after they had taken counsel, they gave large money. . . ." Ah, this is expensive for them, too. ". . . they gave large money unto the soldiers, saying: ' Say ye, His disciples came by night and stole Him away while we slept.' " So their last weapon was a lie and their last policy was deception. It cost them large money to cover up the truth. I would say it was not worth it! In any case, what were those guards doing asleep? They were put there to watch; and on their own confession, presumably, they were asleep! Well, if they hadn't been sleeping, how could Peter and John and Mary, three people, have been able to get into the sepulchre and look round and then Mary and Jesus talk together? They must have been asleep, you see. Or, may be, God sent them to sleep. Elsewhere in Scripture we find the Most High sending people to sleep if it suits Him to do so. They slept, and were paid handsomely to own up that they slept and that the disciples came by night and stole Him away. I am only surprised that Caiaphas did not see the hopeless folly of that. He must have been very tired and jaded! How did they know the disciples had come and taken Him away if they were asleep all the time? Well, they were paid to trump up that tomfoolery. I am sometimes sorry for Satan. To be sure, he does have a job to stifle truth! " And they said, ' If this come to the governor's ears, we will persuade him.' " Caiaphas says: " I've got Pilate just where I want him. If he makes any trouble, it is all right. I'll deal with him and secure you—make you sine cura, without care." Paul says, " I would have you without carefulness "—the same word. " We will rid you of care." That is where I want to leave you on Easter morning. They were promised by a crafty man who paid them well that they could tell their lie and not be afraid, because he would guarantee to keep them without care. I want you to go down the road to-night realising that you have a living Lord who tells you, guarantees to you, that if you believe He is living and tell the truth about Him, He will keep you without care. That is a security I can trust. Then may we obey the injunction of the Easter morning angels and go and tell—*HE LIVES*!

Chapter Three

EASTER AFTERNOON

Reading: Luke xxiv. 13–35 (Revised Version)

COME and walk the Emmaus road with me. Luke is the only one who records this experience in detail. Mark refers to it in one verse, but to Luke we are indebted for all the lovely details of this matchless story. I agree with George Eliot who calls it " The loveliest story in the world ". What makes it so beautiful? Wherein lies the appeal of this story? For, you see, it has to do with the simplest things, the most homely and most undramatic of things. Look! You have a dusty road out to a village;—nothing very romantic in that. And two very ordinary people—not the eleven, just amongst the rank and file of the followers of Jesus, and only one of them is named. You have a talk along the road, the nature of which we shall see in a moment. Nothing very poetic about three people talking along a seven-mile road. You have a country village and a country cottage, a very simple invitation, a very frugal meal; and that is all! Yet out of these homely, ordinary, commonplace materials, the Spirit of God has woven a story which has thrilled folk the world over for best part of two thousand years and which never loses its appeal. Ah, but, of course, we understand why. Into that ordinary dusty road, up to those two ordinary, homely people and into that poor village cottage there comes the Living Lord, and it is He who adds the holy glamour and the heavenly dignity and the divine romance to the tale. The most commonplace walk, the dustiest road, the lowliest home and the most ordinary people can be filled with breathless beauty, with burning glory, and always are so filled, if the Living Lord Himself draws near and takes pre-eminence in the scene. Has Mile End Road been something like that for you to-day? Did Cheapside flame with wonder because Jesus was going with you?

Who were these two people? Cleopas was the name of one. We should like to know who the other was. I always thought it was two men (in common with most people), until I read of Cleophas in John xix. 25 as being the husband of one of the Marys who was faithful to the last to Jesus. Though I must admit the scholars are not unanimous in this matter, it is not improbable that Cleophas and Cleopas are the same person and that these two therefore were husband and wife. When I read of their conversation with their new Friend in verses 19 to 24, I feel pretty sure that the other one was a woman. I think we can see just where the woman speaks. Then when they get home, it is a womanly touch, isn't it? which says: " Now don't go further: you come and spend the night with us. It is very late." That sounds like a woman and a wife. Shall we then for the purpose of this study take for granted that this theory is true and that it is husband and wife trudging home together to their little cottage in the country village of Emmaus?

OUT OF DOORS

My first heading in this section is going to seem to you to be out of place, but I am going to vindicate the choice of the word immediately—

INVESTIGATION. Yes, investigation: because, you see, that is what they were making. You will notice if you read from the Revised Version, that " talked together " in verse 14 and " communed together " in the next verse are the same word in the original and the Revisers keep to the same expression: " They communed with each other." Now what the Saviour says to them in verse 17 throws light upon their communing with each other. He says: " What communications are these that ye have one with another? "; but the word He uses literally means " to throw back and forth ". Have you ever played tennis or ping-pong or badminton or even

" catch "? Well, that is the word: " to throw back and forth "
—as we should say: " What are these things that you are
bandying about one from the other? " Weymouth and
Moffatt both use the same words, the expressions meaning
" conversation " and " discussion ". So what were they doing?
They were thrashing out the things that had happened. Cleopas
would advance one explanation and Mary would bandy back
another. They were thrashing out together the things that had
happened. " Investigation " I think is the word, isn't it?

You see, they had come from the upper room. They had
had their lunch there, and then in the afternoon they had set
out for home. There was nothing else to do. They had spent
the Sabbath in the city as loyal Jews; and now that the
Sabbath restraint was over, and really there was nothing to
wait for, they were going home. Mary had been to the
sepulchre with some of the other women, Peter and John had
been there; the women had come back with stories of angels,
but the men for the most part had dismissed them as " just
these excitable women "; they believed them not. " Idle tales "
is how Luke describes them, and that is the doctor's word
which means " the ravings of delirium ". There was no belief
in the Upper Room—not at this point of Easter afternoon;
it came later. We shall see in due course how it came. But
at the moment they were bewildered, upset: and I imagine
that the prevailing feeling was, except in the mind of John
who believed, that somebody had rifled the tomb and stolen
the body away.

You know how sometimes you desperately want to get to
your own home. There is no place like home, especially when
you are distracted. And you know how, sometimes, when
terrible things have happened you want to get away from it
all. Sometimes you want to get away from other people, too.
I imagine Mary and Cleopas were thinking like this: they
wanted to get home; they wanted to get away from the city;
they wanted to get away from those other people, even their
Christian friends. But they could not get away from their
problem. All the way home, until something happened,
they were bandying to one another the enquiries and the

explanations and the theories and the suggestions and the sup-
positions and whatnot and so on and so forth. Investigation!
Then comes the second—

INTRUSION. One of the loveliest things in the gospels:
"Jesus Himself drew near and went with them." A dear
friend of mine I knew was infirm and not at all in good health
during the blitz on East London. Once, in answer to my
enquiry: "How do you get on when you have to be out in
the blitz?" he said: "Well, I remember a text that Pastor
Moore preached about: 'Jesus Himself drew near and went
with them.' And," said he, "that gets me through all right."
I have never ceased to remember that when I come to this
lovely word in verse 15. Ah, but you haven't really got it
unless you have read it in the Greek, because, you see, these
tenses are in the imperfect. I have lots of "imperfects" to-
night and you must be patient enough to understand them.
You know the imperfect tense, don't you? It is the tense of
going on and on and on and on. Now literally it is that *while*
they were communing together and *while* they were reasoning, Jesus Himself drew near and went with them. The glint of
meaning in the Greek, which it is impossible to reproduce in
the English, is this: so absorbed were they in the conversation that He was walking with them before they knew it.
They did not hear His footfall. They failed to observe that
there was Someone walking by their side. He was there and
He was going with them before they knew that anybody had
joined them.

Intrusion! Yes, it was an intrusion. But, of course, they
never thought of it as such. Haven't you found that sometimes? How He loves to intrude into our dark problems!
But this is what we read of them in verse 16: "Their eyes were
holden that they should not know Him." I cannot explain
that. I only ask you to notice just what is said. Some suggest
that He was different when He rose from the dead, so different
that people did not recognise Him. I don't know about that.
We are not given any clear guidance in the New Testament.
I only know that in this case it was not that, for we are told

that they were deliberately prevented from recognising Him. I imagine that there was something miraculous about that. It was not His will yet that they should know who had joined them. The reason was not in Him, but in them. It was not that He was changed, but that they were holden.

He said unto them: " What are you talking about? " And they stood still, looking sad. Did you notice that in the Revised Version? Just a graphic touch which is slightly more accurate in detail than the Authorised Version. " They stood still, looking sad." It is a pathetic word, that, for " sad " really means " dreary ". It is the downcast look of settled grief. It is the look on the face of a person who says: " I'll never smile again." It is the word Jesus used—it only occurs twice in the New Testament—when He said: " When you fast, be not of a sad countenance. Don't put on a sort of settled gloom, like the Pharisees wear; " and, in the language of the day and the usage of the word, it has in it the aspect of sullenness. Luther translates " sour ". It only brings out the pathos of the story. He is asking them, " What are you talking about? " and they are so amazed that anybody should ask that, that they stand still, looking sad. Have you imagination enough to picture it and see their faces?

And one of them, Cleopas, answering said unto Him . . . Well, what did he say? He said this: " Are you such a stranger in Jerusalem and are you living so quite alone that you do not know what has happened during the last few days? " That is what made them stand still. " Can it be," says Cleopas, " that anybody who has come from the city should not know what has been happening there recently? " There is no resentment, you see, only astonishment. It speaks well for the charm of Jesus that He could so intrude upon the private conversation of man and wife, ask them what they were talking about, go with them, and yet not evoke any resentment. What a charming way Jesus must have had with Him! They did not know who He was yet: He was only a " stranger ", but He could take that liberty and be on friendly terms at once. When I think of these things I do covet that nice way of getting in a word for Him. How lovely to be able to do that in a railway carriage or walking along a pavement! Do you covet that gift? I do.

My friend, here is a lovely glint of the humour of God. You will never convince me that Jesus hadn't a sparkle in His eye. You will never convince me that I won't hear my Saviour laugh heartily when I meet Him in Heaven! Look at this. " And He said unto them: ' What things? ' " Fancy *Him* saying that! Of course, they were so absorbed in their grief that they failed to see the twinkle in His eye, failed to catch the tone of His voice. I am sure there must have been ripples of laughter very near His lips when He said: " What things? "

Oh, and then—I love this—look what they said to Him! I am so glad, because you know, if later on their hearts burned within them as He walked with them by the way, I am sure that here *His* heart burned within *Him* as *they* talked to *Him* by the way. I so admire what they said about Him. Verse 19. They are going to tell Him what things. " Concerning Jesus of Nazareth, which was a prophet, mighty in deed and word before God and all the people." You know, that is a great thing to say of Somebody who has been crucified as a common criminal. That is a noble description of a Man accursed because He has hung upon a tree! It reveals what the disciples thought of Jesus at that time. It was a very limited conception, but no doubt it was fairly representative of them all.

What then did they think of Jesus before they knew He was risen? First of all this means that they had unbounded admiration of Him and affection for Him. They were speaking so highly of Him. His heart must have rejoiced to think that even though they believed Him dead and His cause an utter, dismal failure, yet they could still give such a glowing testimony about Him to a stranger. I notice that it was His miracles which impressed them more than His teaching, if we can go by what they said. " Mighty in *deed* and word "— you notice that they put the deeds first. I think I would have put the words first and the deeds after, but they put the deeds first, then the words. I notice, too, that He meant nothing more to them than a prophet. They should have known that

D

He was far more than a prophet, but that is all He was to them.

But most significant of all: "Concerning Jesus of Nazareth." Is that all they have to say about Him? He was that, but He was more than that. What about Caesarea Philippi? What about Peter's confession: " Thou art the Christ, the Messiah? " I should have expected them to have thought of Him as the Messiah. He had told them so, and they had told Him so on more than one occasion. Isn't it then significant that, speaking about Him to a stranger who does not know anything, they only say that He was " Jesus of Nazareth "? Surely in their omission we see into their hearts. " No, no, we did hope that He might have turned out to be the Messiah. We did trust that it was He who should have redeemed Israel; but, of course, we were wrong. It could not have been the Messiah or He would not have died like that." He was just Jesus of Nazareth, a wonderful Man, but no more—a prophet—Jesus. Now I find that amongst the first things Jesus says to them is this: " Ought not *CHRIST* to have suffered these things? " The Saviour immediately corrects their thinking and puts Himself in His rightful position—the Christ. But, of course, after the things that had happened their Messianic dream was all dispelled.

I am glad that in verse 20 they said nothing about Judas. I admire them for that. They just said: " the chief priests and our rulers . . ." It was one of themselves really, but they did not tell that to a stranger. It would be far better if you never ran down your fellow church-members to strangers, far better. So they talked to Him and they told Him. You know, though their hearts had not yet begun to burn within them, I am very sure that they felt better for it. It is amazing how it lightens a burden just to tell the Lord about it. Do you remember after John the Baptist was beheaded we are told in the next verse, " the disciples came and told Jesus ". "A little talk with Jesus makes it right, all right." Well, the children sing that. We know better: it does not make it " right, all right "; but it marvellously helps. My friends, Jesus deliberately drew them out to give him detailed explanations of what had happened.

Having drawn near to them, He then drew them. He made them talk. He made them unburden the whole thing. I am sure He is still of that mind. I am sure Jesus still wants His people to tell Him carefully and in detail everything that has happened. While you are unfolding the whole sad story into His ears, telling Him exactly what you feel, just what you hoped for and just what happened, it does help so much. The beginning of the burning heart, and the beginning of the vision, and the beginning of the transformation is already taking place as they unburden their souls into the hearing of the Lord.

I only pause one moment longer to suggest to you that in what they said from verse 19 to 24 we have two speakers and not one. " *They* said unto Him. . . ." In reading this as our Lesson to-night I changed my tone of voice, to show where Mary took up the thread. You all know these wives— at least, every husband does. It is a physical impossibility for a wife to allow her husband to tell a story without chipping in! I have never known a wife who has been able to resist that wifely vice! If a husband chips in, he is squashed at once! It is the prerogative of the wives to supplement anything that a poor husband has to say! You must have noticed that! Every husband has suffered from it! Well, here it is. " Concerning Jesus of Nazareth, which was a prophet mighty in deed and word before God and all the people . . ." (19) that is Cleopas. " And how the chief priests and our rulers . . ." and so on; (20) there is Mary. But Cleopas is going to get a bit more in, (21a) " But we trusted that it had been He which should have redeemed Israel." That is the same voice again. " And beside all this, to-day is the third day . . ." (21b). That is Mary. Ah, but here is the man; " Yea, and certain women " (22. 23). That is Cleopas, I am sure! But at verse 24 Mary is going to vindicate what the women said: " And certain of them which were with us, went to the sepulchre and found it even as the women had said "—that is the woman. And if I mistake not, it is Cleopas who puts in the last word, " but Him they saw not ". There is the prosaic, matter-of-fact man! Mark it in your Bibles and read it like that the next time you have to read Luke xxiv in public.

Now it is *HIS* turn. " And He said unto them, ' O fools . . . ' " This word " fool " had a softer meaning in 1611: it does not mean what we mean by " fool " now. " Slow at the uptake "—that is exactly it. Slow at the uptake, dullards; literally, without perception, dull-witted. You see, they had read what the prophets had spoken; they were great Bible readers, these two; and they had failed to perceive the application to Christ; they had read their Bibles without understanding. And He says: " You are dull-witted." Oh, but worse than that: " . . . and slow of heart . . . "—that goes deeper: that is in the realm of feeling and moral susceptibility. I so like the way Moffatt puts it: " Slow to believe after *all* that the prophets have spoken." He is gently rebuking them. He is saying, " *You* with your Bibles, *you* ought to have known that the Messiah was to suffer and to enter into His glory. *You* ought not to have been so astonished and so dismayed, after *all* that the prophets have spoken."

My friends, I cannot read this verse without thinking of what Jesus would say to many a Christian if He joined them on the road like this to-day. Surely He would say this same word. He would say: " Look here, you are talking about things that are happening to-day—Hitler—the War—national extremity and international chaos—you are very sad about it all, after *all* that the prophets have spoken! Don't you see that Christ must come to earth a second time and that all this is according to the warnings in God's Word? " Wouldn't He say that to us to-day? Isn't that how the Church is dull-witted and slow of heart to believe all that the prophets have spoken? As the resurrection in their day was the climax of it all for them and the glory, so in our day, I, for one, believe the second advent is going to be the glory and the climax of it all. Ought not we to believe what the prophets have spoken? Yet, you know, it is a painfully small minority of Christian people who believe that Jesus is coming to earth again according to the Scriptures, after *all* that the prophets have said and after *all* that is happening in the world to-day before our very eyes, fulfilling what the prophets have spoken.

I find, moreover, if you want to have a burning heart in

these days you must believe that Christ is coming again and that all that is happening to-day is leading up to that; you must believe that the darker the clouds to-day the brighter the outlook for the Church; you must believe to-day that the more wicked men get under Satan's domination in the world to-day, the nearer is the coming of the Son of Man. It is the Second Adventist who has the burning heart and who has an opened Bible and an opened eye to understand and believe. "Lift up your heads, for your redemption draweth nigh" is one of the most pertinent words from God to Christian people today.

But I am digressing. After intrusion, I find—verse 27—INTERPRETATION. "And beginning at Moses and all the prophets He interpreted. . . ." Did you notice that in the Revised Version, it is better than "expounded", I think; it is warmer. ". . . interpreted unto them in all the Scriptures the things concerning Himself." "The passages in the Scripture which referred to Himself,"—Moffatt and Weymouth together. What a Bible reading in the open air to a congregation of two! I haven't time to discuss it, but beginning at Genesis iii, beginning with the seed of the woman, going on to Mt. Moriah in Abraham's day, the offering up of Isaac, into Exodus, the Passover Lamb, away into Leviticus, the day of Atonement, the scapegoat, to Numbers, Balaam's prophecy, the sceptre, the star, do you remember it? Touching many points in Deuteronomy, no doubt, on into David, some of the Psalms which spoke of Him. And Isaiah! I wonder what Jesus said about "the virgin shall conceive"? I wonder what He said about "the Son—given" in the ninth chapter? I wonder what He said about chapter liii, and those later chapters of Isaiah which all speak of Himself,—I wonder how He put them? What a Bible reading! On into Jeremiah, into Ezekiel—oh, how Ezekiel must have flamed and flashed as He interpreted it concerning Himself! Then right through the Minor Prophets. Were the Minor Prophets dull? Did they shrug their shoulders and fidget whenever in the synagogue the exposition was in the Minor Prophets? My word!

They got *THE* Minor Prophets that day! I wonder how often they stopped to consult the scroll they were carrying! I wonder how long it took them to cover the rest of the seven miles because they just couldn't walk, they were so intrigued. "In all the Scriptures the things concerning Himself." Finishing up in Zechariah, "the bells upon the horses". Oh, what a Bible reading! Concluding finally in Malachi: "and the Sun of Righteousness shall arise with healing in His wings." What a Bible reading! Can you imagine it? No wonder their hearts burned!

But, look, they are home now. "He made as though He would have gone further." But they constrained Him, pressed Him. Here's a guest they really wanted to stay. You don't press all your guests to spend the night with you. Sometimes you fervently wish that they would go! But here they press Him and not so much for their sakes as for His. "You can't go on; it is getting dark; there are robbers on this road; come in; come in with us." Lyte's hymn, founded on this verse, is really the reverse idea of this verse. Exquisite and immortal as the hymn is, Lyte sings: "Abide with *me*, fast falls the eventide." He is thinking solely of his own need. But what the Emmaus couple said was, "Abide with *us*". Cannot we minister to Thee? They were thinking only of Him. So the fourth heading is—

INVITATION. He loves to be invited. There is nothing pleases Jesus more—nothing pleases Him so much—as being constrained, and it is when we are most eager to keep Him with us that He most deeply abides with us. Says Dr. Maclaren: "Jesus forces His company on no one. He would have gone further if they had not said, "Abide with us". He will leave us if we do not keep Him, but He delights to be held by beseeching hands, and our wishes constrain Him. Happy are they who, having felt the sweetness of walking with Him on the weary road, seek Him to bless their leisure and to add a more blissful depth of repose to their rest."

"And He went in, to tarry with them." Alexander Maclaren has another gem here: "The Christ who is asked to come in order to receive, abides in order to bestow." So much then for out of doors. Now for—

INDOORS

What do we find? First:

DISTRIBUTION. They are round their table now. " As He sat at meat with them." Is Jesus always recognised at your table? Well, He is there. But it is the happy home which recognises Him and always remembers He is there. I think sometimes the spreading of the table would be different if it were remembered that He is there. I am sure we should not be so extravagant sometimes. Our conversation at the meal table would be different if we remembered that He sits at meat still with His own. Half-way through the meal, in that charming way of His that no one could be offended with, He quietly assumed the position of host. He took the loaf and blessed it and brake and gave to them. Distribution! And here's another imperfect: literally it is " He was giving to them "—in the act of giving them the broken bread—and the second thing happens—

DISCOVERY. " Their eyes were opened." The distribution led to the discovery. Later on they told that " He was known of them in the breaking of the bread ". Now, they had not been at the Upper Room. They had not been at the Communion Service. They were not amongst the number of the twelve. But they had heard about it. They may have been at the feeding of the five thousand, and then at the feeding of the four thousand. Anyway, it was something to do with the distribution of the loaf that led to the discovery. It was either the way in which He brake and gave that made them recognise Him; or else it was that, as He gave it to them in His outstretched hand and they took the piece of bread,—" Why, there's the scar! " And they knew Him; and, immediately, the third thing in this second half—

DISAPPEARANCE. He was gone! Well, I don't know that that is right. I am not sure that it is right to say that He was gone, because the literal rendering of the Greek is: " He ceased to be seen of them." Disappearance, dis-appearance, you see? He may have been there still, but they did not see Him. Oh, that is hard! At the very moment of recognition He becomes invisible. Well, yes—it may have been hard but, you see, He is going away altogether very soon and they have got to get used to the new order of things entirely, depending no longer on His physical appearance but on His spiritual presence. So I always think that these occasional appearances and disappearances after Easter are to get the disciples gradually into the way of doing without Him altogether. He never stayed long with them. Now that He has manifested Himself alive by this infallible proof, He disappears. What then?

DECLARATION. Look, they are off! That very hour they are off to tell the others. They have tramped seven and a half miles out of Jerusalem; they are dead weary with all their travel and excitement; but, oh, " It is towards evening; it is dark; there are robbers on the road, but, Mary, I must go back," Cleopas says. " Let me go back and tell the others that He is alive, Mary. I *must* let the others know." " You aren't going alone: I'm going with you," Mary replies. " I'm going, Cleopas, it's no use saying me nay. If you go, you must let me go with you." So they went together to declare what they had come to know. It may be there are Christians here to-night who have never gone seven yards out of their way, let alone seven miles, to tell of what they know about a living, loving Saviour.

So they get back to the Upper Room that night, only to find that their journey was not really necessary! They need not have gone at all. What met them in that Upper Room was this: " The Lord is risen *indeed.* . . ." Oh, so *they* know now —" indeed "—no doubt about that! What has happened? " And hath appeared unto Simon."

It was the appearance to Simon which made the rest of

the disciples know *indeed* that Jesus was risen. I doubt if Peter ever told the others what transpired between him and the Lord that afternoon. The Gospels give no hint, nor Peter's two Epistles; and all Paul says is " After that, He was seen of Cephas, then of the twelve ". I don't think Peter will ever tell us. I don't think it will be fair to ask him. What goes on between a backslider and the restoring Lord is not for public hearing. There are some things not lawful to be uttered, and this is one of them. But I know this: Peter was so vastly changed that they could disbelieve the resurrection no longer. That *indeed* still depends upon a transformed disciple. We shall never convince the world that Jesus lives unless and until we can show them ourselves so completely different that they will know that a living Saviour is the only explanation. I want to say this: there may be deniers here; I may be speaking to grievous backsliders; I may be speaking to men and women who have been damaging the cause of Christ by their daily living at work, at home; nobody believes in Jesus because of them, they are so completely inconsistent, so frequently denying, so utterly backsliding. Listen! If you can go back home now and to work to-morrow as transformed as Simon Peter was on Easter Day, they will believe that Jesus is alive!

Chapter Four

EASTER EVENING

Readings Luke xxiv. 35–48: John xx. 19–23

WILL you come with me to a room in Jerusalem to-night? We are not quite sure which room it is, but probably it is that upper room at which the Passover was eaten and the Communion Service of the Christian Church instituted, the home of John Mark, the headquarters of the Early Church, the room perhaps into which the Holy Spirit was sent on the day of Pentecost. It is to this room of memories we must make our way in Jerusalem to-night.

The day is far spent and the evening shadows are falling. The disciples are assembled—not just the eleven (or rather ten, because Thomas was not there and Judas had gone)—but also, Luke tells us, " those that were with them ". Unless I am very much mistaken, John and Mary Magdalene had been spending the greater part of the day rounding up all the friends of Jesus, saying to them: " Now you must come to the upper room this evening. Strange things have been happening to-day and we must all keep together."

So, as the evening gathers in, from every direction the followers of Jesus make their way to this by now well-loved room, " a large upper room furnished ". John Mark's father and mother are giving no doubt their customary lavish hospitality. They have been broiling some fish and they have been out to the beehives gathering honey to make a meal for what was probably a considerable company. I don't know quite what they were talking about, or what exactly was their mood. I think they were badly frightened, very disturbed and, sorrowfully enough, hard of heart. So much so, that when their Lord appeared to them later on, one of the first things He

did was to upbraid them for their unbelief and hardness of
heart because they would not believe those who had seen Him
that morning alive from the dead. You remember, the reports
of the women, Mary Magdalene and the others, appeared as
idle tales and the men would not believe.

If we could have been in that room there that evening, I
should like to have seen the faces of three people especially.
I should like to have seen the face of John, because it would
have been a haven of rest. John, you remember, believed
when he saw the linen clothes lying in the tomb in the morning; he saw, and we noticed that the Greek word is " to
see with perception "; he understood and believed. So there
was no doubt in John's mind that the Master was really risen
from the dead.

I should like to have seen the face of Mary Magdalene, the
first to see Him risen. She was convinced. An excitable
woman, so excitable that she could never convince the others,
—they had a prejudice against Mary. " Oh, she's hysterical,"
they would say. She was a great woman for all that. You
remember that once upon a time seven devils had lived within
Mary.

I should like most of all to have seen the face of Simon
Peter, though I don't think I would have been able to see his
face for very long—for his tears and for mine. It was the fact
that Simon Peter was so utterly transformed that those
gathered together were really beginning to be convinced.
Their testimony you remember was: " The Lord is risen indeed and hath appeared unto Simon." I notice, by the way,
that angels are kinder than men. When the angels referred
to the denier, they said: " Go and tell His disciples and Peter."
They were kind enough to use his new name. I dare say the
Risen Lord had particularly instructed them about this. When
the disciples referred to him, however, they used the old name
" Simon ", as though to say: " You can't call him ' Peter ' after
what happened on Friday morning." But Peter had met the
Lord and there was such a difference in him that they knew
Christ was risen indeed. That was all they knew. They did
not know where He was, and, though they were convinced

of the fact that He was living and out of the tomb, there was still a good deal of questioning in their minds.

Look at the doors: they are barricaded. Every bolt is in its place; I think they must have pushed furniture against the doors! They are prepared for an invasion! The doors are shut " for fear of the Jews ". I wonder what they were frightened of? Do you think they were frightened that perhaps some of the Jewish authorities would proceed to take them also? I don't think that was likely. Caiaphas and Pilate were quite satisfied. I think they had no further interest at the moment in those followers of the Nazarene. After Pentecost they were going to give anything in their kingdom to arrest the ring-leaders. I wonder if the disciples had heard what Caiaphas had paid those sleeping soldiers to tell. I wonder if they knew that it was spreading about the city that they had stolen the body out of the tomb. I wonder if they feared a rush of police to arrest them. Maybe that was what made them fear and bolt the doors. I wonder whether they feared a mob, a riot on behalf of some of the people of Jerusalem. You remember, in Acts xvii we are told how some of the Jews hired " lewd fellows of the baser sort " to stir up the people and they mobbed the house of Jason and took him away into custody. I wonder if the disciples feared a riot like that? Anyway, they were frightened and the doors were barricaded and they were together talking, querying, wondering.

Listen! There are footsteps on the stairs! Who is this? Every face pales! Two stairs at a time! People leaping up the stairs! Is this the police? A loud imperious knock on the door! " What shall we do?" Probably only John is really calm, and he calms the rest. " Who is it?" Again that knocking at the door. Then a familiar voice, and a sigh of relief from the company. " Oh, it's only old Cleopas! What's he doing? Why, he has gone back home to Emmaus with Mary! What's he doing?" They take down the barricade and let in Cleopas and Mary, all travel-stained and hot and flushed with excitement. Before they are through the door, they cry: " We have seen Him! He has had supper with us! It's all true! " They come in and are told of the new events since they left this afternoon for Emmaus—what has happened to Simon.

The two travellers sit down, and Luke tells us, they rehearse at length (for that is what the word means) all that has happened and how He was known to them in the breaking of the bread. Full of it—both of them talking at once! You know how Cleopas and Mary butted in on one another in speaking to the Stranger on the road. You may be sure that it was a duet in the upper room—both of them talking at once, giving the whole story, Mary filling in one detail, Cleopas chiming in with another!

Suddenly, the excited talking of the two and the babel of exclamations and comments from the rest perish in an instant and gasp into silence. He is there!

All are thunderstruck, spellbound, silent! He is there! Yet, oh it is not He! Horrors! It is not He: it is His ghost! Over-wrought as they were, their nerves jangled, tired and frightened, the women screamed, the men paled! Only for a moment, however, only for a moment. Then that voice, that dear voice of His, in the old familiar greeting: " Peace be unto you." Still they cannot believe it. Luke says they could not believe it " for joy ". It is too good to be true. Oh, Master!

On Easter evening, after He had come, He did three things. First of all, He convinced them that it was really He Himself; secondly, He clarified their minds about the whole business, opened the Scripture and opened their hearts to receive it; and thirdly, He commissioned them. Or, shall I put it for you in this way for easier remembering? He gave them three priceless blessings: He gave them Assurance; He gave them Apprehension; and He gave them Authority.

I

ASSURANCE. The first thing He did was to assure them that it was really He. John writing long after, does not dwell on that because Luke had given it in detail. So we will begin in Luke xxiv; and you will find that from verse 36 away down to verse 43 Luke is telling us of how Jesus convinced them, gave them assurance. It is very beautiful, well worth dwelling on.

You may well ask why they were so frightened. Apparently they were convinced that He was alive. They had heard from several that He had been seen by them. Ah, I'll tell you what created the difficulty and the fright. He had not come through the door! Half an hour before they had taken down the barricade and shot back the bolts to let in Cleopas and Mary. But He had come without anyone raising a finger. He could not have come through the window, for it was an upper room. And they knew He had not come through the door. He was just suddenly there.

I don't believe He had come at all. I believe He had been there a long time; and just at the right moment He made them aware of His presence. He had the power of doing that, though before He seldom used that power. You see, that is why they were frightened, and what He had to conquer in their nerve-strained minds was the delusion that He was a ghost. He had to convince them that He was real. So He said to them, (verse 38) speaking in gentle tones of rebuke: " Why are ye troubled and why do thoughts . . . " . . . " reasonings " in the Revised Version: literally " dialogues " . . . " why do dialogues arise in your hearts? " Have you ever had a dialogue in your heart? One moment your heart is saying " It is true "; the next moment your heart is saying " It can't be true. Don't be silly! " Dialogues in the heart! I think I would like to preach about that one day. It would be a great subject, with a bit of sanctified psychology in it! But, you see, He is saying to them in effect: " Why are you reasoning about a matter concerning which your spiritual perception ought to have convinced you? There ought to be something in your heart which tells you that it is I, even if for the moment your head cannot follow it. Behold My hands and My feet that it is I myself. Handle Me and see."

" Handle Me and see." We must go back for a moment to see what John wrote, years later. " That which was from the beginning, which we have heard, which we have seen with our eyes, which we beheld, and our hands handled, concerning the Word of life." Was John thinking of this moment when he wrote that at the beginning of his epistle? Ah, they touched Him, they heard Him, they handled Him, they took hold of Him. Yes! yes! He was solid enough. He was real. There was no ghost about Him.

I cannot help feeling interested in what He said. "A spirit hath not flesh and bones as ye see Me have." Now the common expression for humanity was "flesh and blood". "Flesh and blood hath not revealed it unto thee, but My Father which is in Heaven." Is there any significance in the fact that Jesus said "flesh and bones"? Did it mean that this resurrection body of His was bloodless? Blood is the life: does it mean, then, that our resurrection bodies are going to be bloodless— that blood which gives life to our present human, mortal frame is the sign of earthliness; and that one mark of heavenly bodies is that they have no blood? I wonder. "Flesh and bones." A queer way of putting it, don't you think? or isn't there any significance in it? If there is, I can understand why He was taken for a ghost, because flesh and bone would be pale, deathly, bloodless, ghostlike. I wonder. We must ask about that when we get to Glory.

"And when He had thus spoken He showed them His hands and his feet." John put it later on in his gospel: "Then were the disciples glad when they saw the Lord." The word he used there is the same word he used of himself earlier in the chapter—earlier that day, at the time when he saw and believed. They were glad because now they saw with perception, they understood, they believed, they were convinced.

At a recent Baptist Union Assembly the Missionary Sermon was preached by our own Rev. B. Grey Griffith, B.D., an ex-President of the Baptist Union. It was a great sermon! One of the notable things he said in that sermon was this: that very few of Christ's disciples ever saw His wounds. Well, didn't they see the wounds here? No, no! They did not see the wounds: they only saw the scars. Grey Griffith is right. There is a great deal of difference between a wound and a scar. These were merely scars, *wounds that had been healed*. John saw the wounds. The Marys—the Magdalene and the other Mary—the virgin Mother, saw the wounds. The dripping, bleeding, open wounds with the flies on them! But now the wounds are healed and they merely see the scars. Then, of course, I must ever keep in mind as I think of this that in Heaven at this moment they are looking upon those same scars. When you and I see Him, whether it be in the Glory or whether it be first in the skies, we shall know Him by the print of the nails in His hands. We are going to see those scars, but we shall never see the wounds. Luke was naturally interested in this, being a doctor.

Luke has not finished yet. At verse 41 he says: " While they yet believed not for joy." He gave them another proof. He said: " Have you here any meat? " And they gave Him a piece of a broiled fish and of an honeycomb." I cannot help smiling! It sounds like war-time austerity, doesn't it? " Have you any meat? " " Well no, but there is some fish and a bit of honey! " But it does not mean that. Literally it means: " Have you anything eatable? " They still need a little more proof to be thoroughly convinced and at rest; and so His wit suggests to Him that a spirit could not eat a meal. As they bring to Him the remainder of the feast prepared by the good man of the house, He takes the fish and the honeycomb and " He did eat before them". Not, of course, that He needed any food. He was not hungry—He had a spirit-body incapable of hunger— but He made Himself able to assimilate food in order to give them yet another infallible proof, by which, as Luke says in the Acts, He showed Himself alive after His passion. Thus He gives them Assurance. They all know now that it is really their Risen Lord.

I must just say a word, before passing on, about that body of the Lord. I do not say that I can explain it; I don't think anybody can explain it or even understand it. I think we can never understand an infinite thing such as a resurrection body with our present finite comprehension; but I do think there is a word in 1 Corinthians xv which throws light upon the matter, verses 40 and 44. Paul, you remember, is speaking about the resurrection body, of which the body of Jesus on Easter Day is the first fruits. " There are also celestial bodies and bodies terrestrial; "—that is to day, bodies for Heaven and bodies for earth—" but the glory of the celestial is one, and glory of the terrestrial is another." Then this: " It is sown a natural body, it is raised a spiritual body. There is a natural body and there is a spiritual body." Now surely that helps. Before Jesus died He had a natural body; after He rose He had a spiritual body. The natural body up to Calvary was for terrestrial use; the spiritual body after Easter was for celestial use. It will be so with us. For He is the " firstfruits of them that sleep ". At the moment, you see, we have a body which is adaptable for the earthly condition. It is a limited body, a corruptible body, a mortal body. But when Jesus comes again and the resurrection of the righteous takes place, we are going to have a Heavenly body, adapted for Heavenly use. It is going to be unlimited, incorruptible, immortal. Now Jesus rose from the dead in that Heavenly spiritual body. That explains the difference there was between Him before the grave and after. Different, and yet it was the same dear Lord.

II

APPREHENSION. His second benefit to them was apprehension. He clarified their minds, as I said, about the whole thing. He repeated the open-air sermon on the Emmaus Road to the whole company gathered in the upper room. Luke goes on—at verse 44—" He said unto them, These are the words which I spake unto you, while I was yet with you . . . "—that indicates the difference, you see: " While I was yet with you "—I am not with you now, not as I was— " that all things must be fulfilled which were written."—and here are the three great divisions of the Hebrew Scriptures— " in the law of Moses, in the prophets, and in the psalms concerning Me." Every part of the Old Testament is really about Christ. He Himself said so. Christ is the one great subject of the whole Bible.

Now look at the next verse—(45)—" Then opened He their understanding that they might understand the Scriptures." That word " opened " means, literally, " to open up thor-

E

oughly ". I like the word Dr. Campbell Morgan suggests:
" disentangle ". Very graphic, that. That is what He did for
them. He had done it to Cleopas and Mary and made their
hearts burn; now He does it for the others, He disentangled
their thinking about Himself; straightened out their problem
for them; showed them what He had shown on the way to
Emmaus, that the Messiah was to suffer and enter into His
glory, and how everything in the Old Testament was a
picture, a shadow of Himself; and how He had fulfilled it all.
Yes, He disentangled them: made them see it all in the right
focus; solved their doubts; clarified their problems. In other
words, He gave them apprehension. I think that is the word,
for to apprehend a thing means to grasp it with the mind, to
take hold of it. After that Bible reading in the upper room
that night, they were able to take hold of the whole thing.
In short, Christ gave them a new Bible. I hope you see Christ
in all the Scriptures from Genesis to Revelation. I shall never
forget when I first realised that. It gave me a new Bible, and
I have gloried in that apprehension ever since.

III

AUTHORITY. Finally, He gave them authority. For this
we must turn away from Luke to John. John xx. 21. " Then
said Jesus to them again, Peace be unto you; as My Father
hath sent Me, even so send I you. And when He had said this,
He breathed on them, and said unto them, Take ye holy
breath. Whose soever sins ye remit, they are remitted unto
them: and whose soever sins ye retain, they are retained."

He gave them their authority. What do I mean by that?
As Bible scholars you must be patient while I explain the
wealth of these words. Most of you will be familiar with
the fact that the two words for " send " in verse 21 are not the
same word in the Greek. It is our poor old English breaking
down again! You cannot put it into English. The use of these
two separate words is extraordinarily significant and sugges-
tive. The word He says first—As My Father hath sent
Me . . .—is the word which gives us our word " apostle "—

the Greek word " apostello "; the second word He uses—
" even so send I you," is a more ordinary word for sending:
" pempo ". Christ sent by the Father: apostello; the disciples
sent by Christ: pempo. Now why does Jesus not use the same
word about Himself and His mission for His disciples and
their mission? For this very good reason. The word He uses
about His own mission, apostello, literally means " to send
away " and it is always the word of delegated authority. It is
the word of the ambassador. Lord Halifax was despatched
to Washington with the authority of King George and the
British Parliament delegated to him; and the representative
of the Crown and of the State in America is Lord Halifax—
delegated authority. The ambassador goes away and the one
who has sent him stays behind. This is " apostello ". But
" pempo " is less honourable—a noble word—not dishonour-
able or ignoble, of course—but it has not the same dignity as
the first word " apostello ". " Pempo " is never delegated
authority, but to despatch under authority. The Sergeant-
Major sends the N.C.O. with a message to the Commander-
in-Chief, let us say. Well, that is just to despatch a message.
That is not an envoy; that is not the rank of an ambassador.
That is a man despatched under authority. Poor illustrations,
but they will give you some understanding and insight into
these two words.

Now do you see the significance of this? One of the
greatest things Jesus ever claimed for Himself was that He
was the Sent of God, that He was God's own representative
on earth, the Ambassador from the Most High to this world.
He claimed, moreover, that all God's authority was in his own
hands; that when He spoke, God spoke; as when Lord Halifax
speaks in Washington King George and Winston Churchill
are speaking, for Lord Halifax goes with a direct message
from the Crown or from the State. So at Bethlehem, the
Father, in the person of God the Son, came to earth: Christ
the Divine Ambassador, the One with delegated authority.
Not so does Christ send out you and me. We are despatched
under authority. He does not delegate His authority to us
His messengers: He retains His authority but He sends us out

with all the strength and power of it; and we are to carry out His enterprises here on earth. He has the authority and we work under it. That is the difference.

Here is also another point of difference. " Apostello "—is generally used of anyone sent alone. " Pempo " is generally used for anyone sent with an escort. When the Father sent the Son to be the Saviour of the world, He sent Him alone. Jesus had no one else to accompany Him. He is the only Saviour, and must ever stand alone. When we are sent out as His messengers we never go alone: we are always under escort: Divine escort. " And they went forth everywhere, *the Lord working with them* "—they were escorted: the Holy Ghost accompanied them. The Holy Ghost accompanies us; we never go alone. Under His authority and accompanied by the Spirit of God we go, sent by Christ. That is our commission. Not for ministers, not for Church secretaries, not for archbishops, not for popes, but for you. Every humble believer in Jesus Christ. There is no apostolic succession in this dignity, save as every believer everywhere joins in the dignity and glory of the succession.

Now what are we to do? What are you to do as a humble Christian to-day? Verse 23. " Whose soever sins ye remit, they are remitted unto them; and whose soever sins ye retain, they are retained." What havoc the Church of Rome has made of this! A great deal of priestcraft and popery has arisen out of this verse, but they forget that this was not said to the apostles: it was said to the general run of the believers— " the eleven and those that were with them! " Does that mean then that you, any of you, can remit a person's sin or retain a person's sin? Of course it does. You are going to pay a soul-winning call to-morrow, are you? You are going to call in on a neighbour—just an ordinary neighbour and you an ordinary believer; you have no authority from any church; you are not a church worker; you don't wear any ecclesiastical uniform; you are just an ordinary church member; and you are going to pay a call to win a soul for Christ in a neighbour's house to-morrow night. You are going to take your Bible with you and you are going to get your neighbour on her knees and you are going to kneel by her side—you two women, let us suppose, a Christian and a non-Christian. Now that neighbour of yours to-morrow night is going to believe the Scriptures. You are going to have the joy of seeing her repent of her sin, believe what you say, what the Bible says about the Cross, and you are going to hear that neighbour say to-morrow night: " I believe that Jesus Christ died for me." And you are going to see evidence in her face that the miracle of conversion has happened. Then you are going to grip her hand and say: " Your sins which are many are all forgiven you." That is not priestcraft. That is you with your Lord's authority saying to a new convert: " You have accepted God's terms: you are a saved soul." You remit her sins. You know that they are all forgiven.

Alas, it may be to-morrow night that neighbour is going to say: " No, I can't see it ", and is going to mean by that: " I won't see it ", and you will discern that it is too big a cost. She is not willing to take her stand amongst her neighbours. There is a husband coming home from abroad in a few months' time, and she feels that she cannot face him and tell him that she is a Christian. So, sick at heart, you bid her " good night", knowing that she has not received the Saviour, knowing that she has spurned God's offer of forgiveness, and you quietly take her hand and you say: " You are yet in your sins. You are not forgiven. You have spurned God's offer of pardon." On your Lord's authority you tell her that her sins are retained.

That is what this means, surely. Every believer is sent and escorted to talk to the world about sin. Yes, the main duty of the church in the world is to deal with sin. Some churches never hear the word from one year's end to the other. The church is here for the sake of sin. " As My Father hath sent Me . . . " Why did the Father send Him? " Thou shalt call His name Jesus, for He shall save His people from their sins." " Jesus Christ was manifested to take away sin . . . to put away sin by the sacrifice of Himself." He came about *sin*, to deal with sin, to put away sin by the sacrifice of Himself—the Lamb of God to bear away the sin of the world. " As My

Father hath sent Me, even so I despatch you, under the same authority." We are to deal with sin. And you are to do it. Not only I as a minister, nor the Sisters, nor the missionaries, but you. We are all in it. Sent! That is our authority. That is our responsibility.

Thank God for the resources, though! I left out a verse, didn't I? I did it deliberately in order to close with it. " And He breathed on them and said . . ."—prophetically, symbolically, anticipating Pentecost. He said, literally, " Take ye holy breath." They were going to wait in that upper room until they had that Breath within them and then they were going out to warn and win. Beforehand, as an emblem of what He was going to do, before giving them their supreme responsibility, He assured them of their infinite resources. You have that Holy Breath; so have I. God breathed into our souls the breath of life when we were born again, when we were re-created in Christ Jesus. We are living souls! We have it! The Escort is by our side! On the authority of the Lord in Heaven, accompanied by the Divine Escort and in the power of the Holy Breath, let us go and deal with sin in this sinful world!

> " Breathe on me, Breath of God,
>   Fill me with life anew,
> That I may love what Thou dost love,
>   And do what Thou would'st do.
>
> " Breathe on me, Breath of God
>   Till I am wholly Thine,
> Till all this earthly part of me
>   Glows with Thy fire Divine."

CHAPTER FIVE

AN UNBELIEVER AND A DISBELIEVER

Readings: John x. 31–39: xi. 1–16: xiv. 1–6: xx. 24–28

WE have now to think of the Saviour revealing
Himself to two other persons individually. He
has shown Himself to Mary Magdalene and to
Simon Peter. We have studied these two. You are all familiar
with the story of the appearance to Thomas, but did you
realise before that the Saviour just as deliberately and definitely
revealed Himself to His own brother? I want to begin with
him. We are simply told the statement by Paul: " After that,
He was seen of James."

Now I am intrigued with this because, as you know, right
up to this time His own family, apart from His mother, did
not believe in Him. We have evidence in the Gospels of how
they were quite often a thorn in His side. They once wanted
to take Him away for a holiday because they said: " He is
beside Himself." I read in John vii a definite statement that
His brethren did not believe in Him. He had four brothers.
He had at least three sisters; at least three, because we read,
" Are not His sisters ALL here with us? "; if He had only had
two sisters, the word would have been " both ", so there must
have been at least three sisters. His four brothers are named.
Now the eldest brother in the family—the real eldest brother
of the family—begotten of Joseph—next junior to the Saviour
Himself—was James, and James became the Bishop in Jerusalem and the writer of the epistle that bears his name. Some
time after Easter, Jesus deliberately went out of His way to
show Himself alive to His eldest brother, James. I have no
doubt in my own mind that that explains James thereafter.
James, in common with his brothers and sisters, was an
unbeliever right away up to the Cross and beyond it. They

became believers; and there are some who think that we have the names of all of the four brothers in the Acts, that all four, as we should expect, became pillars in the Early Church.

Did you realise that before? I imagine that is one of the things which these detailed Bible studies bring out. I say, did you? Because now I am going to make a confession that until this very day I did not! It has come as a lovely new thing to me. Well, there is one unbeliever. I think we ought to call James an unbeliever, because he had never believed before.

When we come to Thomas we come to a disbeliever, that is to say, one who has believed but has deliberately turned away from it. Now who is this man, Thomas? He is one of the misunderstood characters of the Bible. He is dubbed as a doubter and tradition has done him an irreparable injury: he will never get over it until the Judgment seat of Christ, when all misunderstandings in the church will be cleared up and all the misunderstood vindicated. I am quite sure we shall find then that for two thousand years—as long as the Lord's coming delays—we have misjudged Thomas. We think of him, generally speaking, as merely a phlegmatic disciple who doubted. Ah! that may be true, he may have been old, and he may have doubted: but he was a great soul, a very great soul.

Four times, including the incident in this study, we meet this disciple Thomas in the New Testament, and every time we see him, it is a dark and cloudy day. We never see Thomas on a day of sunshine. He is always in trouble; that is to say, he always appears when troubles are manifest. The first time we meet him is in the list of the twelve disciples. The first time we really meet him to hear him speak is on the way to the grave of Lazarus. There Thomas shows up magnificently. The Saviour is going into Judea, and the disciples say: " But they tried to stone you there! " " You are surely not going back there again to throw your life away! " " I must go and awake Lazarus out of sleep." Thomas said the best thing that any of them said. He said: " Look here, it's no use saying anything: He has made up His mind to go. We all know, of course, that it means He is going to His death—there is no hope of any other result of His going. But if He has made up His mind to go, He will go, and I am going with Him. Let us also go, that we may die with Him!" Well, if that is a pessimist speaking, it is a fine, devoted, splendid quality of pessimism.

Then we meet him in John xiv, the chapter of the questions. The Saviour is answering Peter's query, "Lord, whither goest Thou?" and concludes with the words "And whither I go ye know and the way ye know." Then Thomas flatly contradicts Him. Thomas says: "Lord, we know not whither Thou goest and how can we know the way?" A man in despair. "Lord, you say we know the way: we don't know the way; and Lord, it is worse than that, it is impossible for us to know it."

Then we meet him here after Easter Day. Finally we meet him in John's Epilogue (Chapter xxi) among the six who went fishing with Peter.

Now I think of Thomas pre-eminently as a practical man of affairs. "Well, if He goes to Judea," Thomas says, "He is going to be killed, that is all!" Thomas has thought it out and read the atmosphere of the city concerning the Master and he has no doubt in his own mind that there is only one result of such a journey, things being as they are. He is very practical. John may have said: "Oh well, perhaps He will be able to get Himself out of it." Peter: "Oh, don't worry! Jesus will manage not to be killed." But Thomas is a practical man of affairs. "No," he says, "He will be killed all right."

We find the same attitude in the second reference to Thomas. "Lord, how can we know the way. Lord, we know not the way Thou goest. Lord, I refuse to pretend that I understand these mysteries, when I cannot see any light upon them at all." And we see it here: "Except I see and except I feel, I refuse to believe." I think we all know this type of man. The man who gets on well in business. A Danish sculptor in one of the churches on the Continent has represented Thomas with a rule in his hand, as though he would measure the things of God. Yes, I think that is Thomas.

Then, of course, I think of him as a moody man, an inveterate pessimist, a born sceptic, a natural doubter, constitutionally slow to believe: quick to criticise, very curious to examine. In a way Thomas cannot help himself: he is always looking on the gloomy side of things, always anticipating the worst. Well, my father's second name was " Thomas ", and we used to call him " Didymus ", because we always reckoned he was of that kind, though he was sunny with it. But he used to look on the dark side. If there were two alternatives my father would always choose the worse. He would never say: " Look at the beautiful silver lining to that cloud." If you pointed it out to him he would say: " Look at that great cloud spoiling the silver lining! " It was part of his make-up. Don't be too hard on the Thomases!

Ah, but we have another word to say about Thomas. He was passionately devoted to his Lord. Here is a man who loved Jesus. For a man of his temperament it is no idle thing to say, " Let us also go that we may die with Him ". For a man of Peter's temperament who says glibly: " Though all men forsake Thee, yet will not I ", you know that there is not much in it. But when Thomas says it, then you know that the depths of the man's being are speaking. A practical man of affairs, a born pessimist but a devoutly loyal soul. That is the man we are dealing with.

I always think Tennyson etched the portrait of Thomas in lines he wrote about his friend, Arthur Hallam (In Memoriam, Canto 95);

> Perplext in faith, but pure in deeds,
>   At last he beat his music out.
>   There lives more faith in honest doubt,
> Believe me, than in half the creeds.
>
> He fought his doubts and gather'd strength,
>   He would not make his judgment blind,
>   He faced the spectres of the mind
> And laid them: thus he came at length
> To find a stronger faith his own;
>   And Power was with him in the night
>   Which makes the darkness and the light,
> And dwells not in the light alone.

In this twentieth chapter of John, we are concerned with Thomas on three occasions and we find him in three moods. The first occasion is Easter Sunday evening (24) and we find Thomas absent. The second occasion is some time during that following week (25) and we find Thomas adamant. The third occasion is the next Sunday (26–29) and we find Thomas adoring. Each of these statements about Thomas needs qualifying, however. The point about Thomas's absence is that he was absent *as a disciple*. The point about Thomas being adamant is that he was adamant *in disbelief*. The point about Thomas's adoration is that he was adoring the Deity.

I

THOMAS ABSENT. Verse 24. " But Thomas, one of the twelve, was not with them when Jesus came." I wonder why he was not there. Of course, he may have been ill; he may have been right away out of town; he may have had some prior duty; he may have been quite unable to have been there. But I think it was worse than that. I think he *could* have been there, but he *would* not be. I think the way John puts it implies that he *should* have been there. " Thomas, *one of the twelve*, was not with them when Jesus came." He was not like the two on the road to Emmaus, just the ordinary rank and file of the disciples: he was one of the twelve. There seems to be a hint that there is a dereliction of duty here. Well, what about *you*? Are *you* always there when you ought to be? Am I? It is bad enough when an ordinary member of the church avoidably stops away from a service, but it is worse when one of the responsible officials stays away.

I wonder why he was not there! I think it was not disloyalty. I am sure it was not that. I cannot imagine Thomas ever turning against his Lord. I do not think it was lack of concern: I cannot imagine Thomas indifferent. I do not think it was just because he was cynical.

I think, first of all, it was on account of remorse. I think Thomas remembered what he had said on the way to the tomb of Lazarus; and when the moment of the Saviour's

greatest need had come, Thomas, with the rest, forsook Him
and fled. I can well imagine a man of Thomas's temperament
suffering unutterably over that. He had said he would die with
his Lord, and then, in the moment of testing, he had run away!
" Mine iniquities have taken hold upon me so that I am not
able to look up." Then, I think, with his remorse, there was
just the sheer anguish of what had happened. Probably nobody suffered so much as Thomas when Jesus was crucified,
nor any who felt His sufferings so keenly. See how obsessed
he was by the wounds of his Master: " Except I shall see in
His hands the print of the nails, and put my finger into the
print of the nails, and thrust my hand into His side. . . ." That
sounds like the speech of one who has endured nightmares of
remembrance and who cannot throw off the sight of those
haunting lacerations. For his dearest Friend to have been hurt
like that! And with Thomas's grief would go despair. It had
all come to this! " We trusted that it had been He who should
have redeemed Israel," but instead, the Redeemer of Israel had
been betrayed by Israel to the hated Romans and strung up in
nameless curse on a Roman gibbet. To one of Thomas's
temperament, this was the very end! There was no ray of
hope anywhere. Deep night settled down upon his soul, and
he walked in the outer darkness with a broken heart. In
agony over the whole situation, intensified by his own
failure, Thomas just would not go with the others.

I wonder what he was doing? I wonder if he went to his
Bible? I wonder if, in those depths of anguish, he ever turned
to what in our Bibles is the 42nd Psalm? " My tears have been
my meat day and night, while they continually say unto me:
Where is thy God? When I remember these things I pour
out my soul within me; for I had gone with the multitude;
I went with them to the house of God; with the voice of joy
and praise, with a multitude that kept holyday . . . O my God,
my soul is cast down within me: therefore will I remember
Thee from the land of Jordan. . . ." Wouldn't this just fit
Thomas? " Deep calleth unto deep at the noise of thy water-
spouts: all thy waves and thy billows have gone over me. . . .
As with a sword in my bones, mine enemies reproach me:

while they say daily unto me: Where is thy God? " I wonder if Thomas ever got there in his desolation.

Well, Thomas did the very worst thing that a melancholy man could do. He went away to brood in a corner by himself, hugging his sorrow and his remorse and so exaggerating all his trouble, distorting his outlook. Thomas was the last man to be alone in such a mood. Thomas, more than any of the others, needed human companionship and the touch of a friendly hand. Thomas did what so often *we* do when most we need the help of our friends and our church: we stop away, we brood over it all by ourselves. Someone has said very finely: " Solitude is the mother-country of the strong." Ah, but when we are in trouble, when " sorrows like sea billows roll ", when you are weak through the greatness of your need, then " forsake not the assembling of yourselves together " with the rest. Thomas was not there. What a lot he missed, didn't he? What a lot some of us have missed by not being there. I would like some of you, when you deliberately stay away from a service the next time, to remember Thomas, and then be sure and go, for, at any service, just for you the Lord may come in an entirely new way.

Thomas absent—as a disciple!

II

THOMAS ADAMANT. A week later, when the disciples were together again, Thomas was with them. Something must have happened between the two Sundays. I hope it means that Thomas was missed, that the other disciples went out to find him. Maybe they ought to have found him on the first occasion. Maybe they did, and he refused to come. Well, somehow, during that week, either one or another of them went to him, or, it may be, he came to them. Anyway, " the other disciples therefore said unto him: ' We have seen the Lord.' " Do look out for the absentees—if that is not too Irish! Get into the way of looking round for the folk who are usually there and reporting their absence. Train yourself to miss people.

When they found Thomas, he was in a tantalising mood. "Except I shall see in His hand the print of the nails, and put my fingers into the print of the nails, and thrust my hand into His side, I will not believe." In the Greek it is a double negative: it means, "I will not on any account believe."

When poor Southey's child died, he said: "I will not be taken in again: I will never love any more." I think that is this mood of Thomas. But, mind you, this is sheer defiance. We talk about "doubting Thomas", but Thomas was no doubter: this is far more than doubt: this is dogged disbelief. I want you to notice particularly what he said. He did not say: "If I have the evidence, I will believe." That would be honest doubt. That would be saying: "Oh, I would give anything to believe as you fellows do; and if I could have the evidence that you have had, then I would believe. I want to believe, but I must be convinced." Now Thomas did not say that, nor anything like it. What Thomas said was: "Except I shall see the evidence I will not on any account believe." That is defiance. That is stubbornness. Distinguish carefully between "If I have the evidence, I will believe", implying willingness to be persuaded, and "Unless I have the evidence I won't believe", indicating a determination to be mulish.

Besides, though we have every right to ask for evidence, we have no right to dictate what that evidence is to be. We have no right to say: "Except I can be convinced in my own particular way, I won't believe." There is this also. We should never say: "I *won't* believe." Sometimes, it may be, we have to say: "I can't believe," but we should never say: "I won't believe." We are never to pit our *will* against our belief. I wonder if you follow me here and see that Thomas was not a doubter: he was worse than that: he was a disbeliever, and doggedly so.

And he was cruel with it. I remember that once, in response to request, we published in our Church Magazine a talk which my wife gave to the womenfolk. It was entitled "Mrs. Thomas". I have never forgotten one point in that address that I must confess I rather took to. It was that Thomas, in his disbelief, was cruel and selfish. He was saying in effect:

" I want to take that wounded hand, and I want to put my finger into that wound, I want to see that open side and I want to put my hand right into it "—quite oblivious to the fact that, if he were able to do so, it would bring a lot of pain back to his Lord. And in that little talk Mrs. King pointed out how it was possible, by the disbelief of a disciple, to bring the pain of the wounds back to the Lord. You get a bit callous when you become disbelieving. There is nothing that hardens a soul so much as disbelief.

And you get unreasonable, too. This obstinate attitude made Thomas illogical. So obsessed was he with his grief, so possessed by his remorse, that he was blind to all else. The realist blind to reality! Else he would have seen in a moment the change that had come over the others—their new joy and serenity, the warm springtime that had come upon their wintry despair and how, as someone puts it, a blazing flame was mounting on the hearth that had sunk to ashes. His evidence was there before him—not the hands of the Master, but the faces of the disciples! But he failed to see it. He didn't want to. None so blind as those who won't see!

Thomas adamant—in his disbelief. Yes, Thomas is a grim warning to us.

III

THOMAS ADORING. Then, a few days later, the first Lord's Day evening after Easter Day, Thomas was with them, and Jesus came. Oh, my friends, I do love every verse in the Gospels which shows me the irresistible charm of my Lord! What a Saviour He is! Look: here is a man, one of the twelve, who has let Him down more than once, let Him down by being away from the upper room when He appeared to His own, and who has demanded his own special kind of proof, obstinately, cruelly, unreasonably, a disciple who has incurred the righteous indignation of his Master—What do I find my Lord doing with him? Stinging him with a sharp rebuke? Pointedly ignoring him altogether? Never! I find Jesus giving in to his arrogant conditions and inviting him to do what he has demanded! " Reach hither thy finger, and behold

My hands, and reach hither thy hand, and thrust it into My side." Thomas said: "If I can see, I will believe! No, I won't though: I must be able to touch Him, too." And Jesus accommodates him at every turn. "Behold My hands, Thomas—yes, and reach hither thy finger; put it into the scar; put your hand into My side; never mind Me; I will not mind if it hurts, so long as I can convince you." A charming Saviour!

But I am looking at Thomas. I see Thomas cringing. I see Thomas ashamed, I think; for surely, before the Saviour had finished speaking, Thomas would feel: "How did He know what I said?" Did it dawn on Thomas: "Surely He must have been there all the time, though I never saw Him. He must have heard what I said to the others." You know, if you want to bring healing, restoring shame to the heart of a good man, you repeat to him what he himself has said. What he said in a wild moment you say over to him when he is calm and cool—that will make him very ashamed. Undoubtedly, with the charm, there is mild rebuke, for the very fact that Jesus gives in to Thomas's request means that He is rebuking Thomas for making the request.

But He is still speaking. "And become not faithless, but believing." It is not a question of *evidence*, Thomas, but of *disposition*. Your incredulity is not due to your not having enough ground to warrant your belief, but to your attitude of mind and heart. You are faithless. There is light enough from the sun: it is our eyes that are at fault if we cannot see clearly. "*Become* not faithless." That is it literally. Thomas, by his refusal to believe, is well on the way to becoming faithless. He is well on the way to losing every shred of faith he has ever had. You may think, some of you, that it is a light thing to refuse to believe. You may think that, oh well, you aren't doing anybody any harm by nursing your doubts. But you are! You are putting yourself further and further along the road of becoming faithless. If some Christian people don't stop their dogged, persistent disbelief, their sinful unwillingness to believe, they will find that they will lose their faith. "From him that hath not shall be taken away that

which he seemeth to have." There is warning with the
rebuke: " Become not faithless but believing."

Then what? Did Thomas accept the invitation? No! No!
Thomas was too occupied with adoration. There was something about the way Jesus spoke, something about His presence
there, that brought Thomas to his knees, not now requiring
any evidence but that of his heart. And Thomas, prostrate
now before his Lord, not touching a wound, gets to the
deepest place of faith of any of them. " My Lord, and my
God! " My friends, from Thomas the disbeliever there comes
the greatest and most completely satisfactory and most pro-
found confession of faith in Christ that is found anywhere in
the gospels. Peter at Caesarea Philippi said: " Thou art the
Messiah." That was a great confession, but this is greater.
Did you ever realise before in the gospels that this is the only
time when anybody claimed for Christ Deity, which He often
claimed for Himself. Thomas is saying: " My Lord "—that is
conviction of identity; but he goes on to say (and the Greek
is very emphatic) " and my God "—that is conviction of
Deity. Wonderful Jesus! In a sentence, in the space of thirty
seconds, He transformed a dogged, stubborn, disbeliever into
the greatest believer we have in the four gospels. There is
hope, then, for every Thomas here to-night.

Dorothy Sayers is often a real interpreter. You are familiar
with her play-sequence which the B.B.C. broadcasts, " The
Man Born to be King ". I like nearly all of it except the title.
It is written by a devoted Christian woman who is also a deep
theologian and accomplished student of New Testament
Greek. If you heard the plays on the wireless, you may have
been shocked at the Saviour being personified by an actor,
but you must have realised how wonderful they were. I
remember that they were written for pagans and not for
Christians, and perhaps you can only get to pagans on their
own ground. Well, I think this may prove to be one of the
really great interpretations of the Gospels in our time. Here
is the scene of our present study.

" Now Thomas, called Didymus, was not with the disciples

when Jesus came. And after eight days they were together once more and Thomas with them."

Thomas: You can all say what you like. Seeing's believing. I tell you again—unless I see in His hands the print of the nails—no, seeing's not enough! Until I have felt with my finger the print of the nails—until I grasp and hold Him and thrust my hand into His side, I will believe nothing.

Matthew: Really, Thomas! Anybody'd think you didn't *want* it to be true.

Thomas: Wishful thinking won't do. I want proof. And when I say proof. . . .

John: Hush, Thomas. He is here.

Jesus: Peace be unto you.

Disciples: And to you.

Jesus: Come here, Thomas. Put out your finger and feel My hands. Reach out your hand and thrust it into My side. And doubt no longer but believe.

Thomas: You are my Lord and my God.

Jesus: Thomas, because you have seen Me, you have believed. Blessed are they that have not seen and yet have believed.

Peter, who has suddenly become aware of some appalling implications—

Peter: Master—when I denied You—when we disbelieved and doubted You—when we failed and deserted and betrayed You—is that what we do to God?

Jesus: Yes, Peter.

James: Lord, when they mocked and insulted and spat upon You—when they flogged You—when they howled for Your blood—when they nailed You to the Cross and killed You—is that what we do to God?

Jesus: Yes, James.

John: Beloved, when You patiently suffered all things, and went down to death with all our sins heaped upon You—is that what God does for us?

Jesus: Yes, John. For you and with you and in you when you are freely Mine. For you are not slaves but sons. Free to be false or faithful, free to reject or confess Me, free to crucify God or be crucified with Him."

That is a great interpretation.

" My God ", said Thomas; and then it dawned on the others what that really meant. So Thomas, in becoming convinced, became a strength to the rest.

There is one closing verse. (29). "Jesus said unto him: ' Thomas, because thou hast seen Me thou hast believed. Blessed are they that have not seen and yet have believed.' " His last beatitude! To whom was He speaking? To the other ten? No, surely not, because they *had* seen. No, no, He was thinking of us. His heart was running down the centuries that were to follow; He was thinking of all His friends who, after He had gone back to Heaven, without ever seeing Him, without ever touching Him, would yet believe. In that last beatitude there must be counted you and me: for, as Peter put it long years afterwards, " Whom having not seen ye love, through Whom, though now ye see Him not, yet believing ye rejoice with joy unspeakable and full of glory." Let us be more worthy of that beatitude which includes us, and God help us to be great believers in so great a Lord.

CHAPTER SIX

THE LATER APPEARANCES AND FAREWELL ·

Readings: Matthew xxviii. 16–20; Mark xvi. 19 and 20;
Luke xxiv. 50–53; Acts i. 1–12

IN this chapter we are to think of three occasions on which " He showed Himself alive after His passion by many infallible proofs, being seen of them forty days and speaking of the things pertaining to the Kingdom of God." Amongst all the appearances of the risen Lord after Easter, ten or a dozen of them, we think first of that to the eleven on the mountain in Galilee, the mountain of appointment given by the Lord before He died, ratified by the angels at the open tomb on Easter morning and also ratified by the Lord Himself when He appeared to the women. The account of that appearance we read in the closing verses of Matthew's Gospel. On that occasion He gave to the eleven the great missionary commission. We have next to consider the occasion, not mentioned at all presumably in the Gospels but mentioned by Paul in I Corinthians xv, when He showed Himself to above five hundred brethren at once. And then thirdly we have to consider the occasion, the last one, when to the apostles He showed Himself on Olivet and ascended. It will only be possible to touch lightly on these three occasions.

I

First, then, we go to Matthew. Matthew xxviii. 16. Now I cannot tell you when this was; no one can. It was during those forty days between Easter and Ascension. I imagine it was fairly early after Easter. " Then the eleven disciples went away into Galilee, into a mountain where Jesus had appointed them." Some people think that there were others there, but only the eleven are mentioned, and it seems to me more likely that this was especially for the eleven. But wait a moment—read on. " And when they saw Him they worshipped Him, but some doubted." What! Are they still doubting? Why, even Thomas has been convinced by now! Are they still doubting? Ah, it does not mean that. Let me briefly give you the scene, not so much from the English translation but from the finer reading of the Greek in which Matthew wrote the record.

It was like this. The eleven were gathered at the appointed place, but Jesus had not come. He was not late—He was never late—but according to their reckoning He was late, and He had not come. Peter goes down to the brow of the downs, which commands a view of the path winding up the hillside, to see if He is coming, but there is no sign of Him. Another disciple goes down to see if He is coming and returns, shaking his head. The Master has not arrived. Is He really coming? And suddenly, as before, He is there. He is there—not immediately in their midst, but just a little way from them. He is suddenly there! and no one had seen Him arrive. Of course, as before, it is probable that He had been there all the time and suddenly He made Himself visible to them and they all saw Him. As they looked upon Him suddenly appearing yonder before them, the majesty of His person compelled them to worship. It is the " prostrate " word for worship, the word which means that they were flat on their faces before Him. And in the very act of worshipping, some doubted.

Wavering worshippers! Do you know anything about that? This message seems to me to be always urgent upon Christian people. It is so tragically possible still to worship Christ and yet, in the very act of worshipping Him, to waver. Now this word " doubted " is an unusual word: it only occurs twice in the New Testament and both times are in Matthew. When Peter walked on the water and was saved by his Master, Jesus said unto him: " O thou of little faith! Wherefore didst thou *doubt*?" It is the same word; and it is only on these two occasions, then and there, that this word is used in the New Testament. It means literally " to stand in two ways at once ". I don't think I can illustrate it, but I think you will see what it means. Anyway, you will from Peter walking on the water. One moment he was looking at his Lord, and walking by faith: the next moment he was looking at the waves, and walking in fear. Then again looking at his Lord and receiving strength: but anon a big wave makes him lower his victorious gaze and he is once more frightened and floundering. Wavering—standing in two ways at once—one moment full of faith, the next moment full of fear. A very unsatisfactory way of walking and living! As James says: " he that wavereth is like a wave of the sea, driven with the wind and tossed: let not that man think that he shall receive anything from the Lord."

Ah, then I think I see what this means. I think I can sympathise with them, I think I have done it in my own soul again and again. As they looked at Him standing there suddenly before them, they were compelled to worship, so glorious was He, so commandingly majestic. As some of them lifted their gaze from their prostration on the ground, they looked into His eyes and they saw something that was so challenging there that they knew He had big things for them: they knew that He was calling them to something great: and as they looked at Him, worshipping Him, they shrank, some of them, from what they knew He was going to give to them and demand of them. I think He must have had His flint face on that day. They wavered! Wavering worshippers! Do you not remember some Sunday evening service, some great rally, a missionary meeting, a convention gathering, when the Lord Christ was so exalted before you in the power of the Holy Spirit that you were worshipping Him. There was nothing else for it—you had to worship Him. But did you waver as you worshipped? Perhaps you are not on the Mission Field yet. Perhaps you are still defeated. Perhaps you are yet in your sins. Oh to worship Christ without wavering!

No wonder they wavered! For look what He had to say to them. "Jesus came,"—you see, He came right up to where they were now, came close—" and spake unto them, saying "

—and, Oh, what a word is this! You have noticed the four
" alls"? " ALL power is given unto Me in Heaven and on
earth. Therefore go ye and disciple ALL nations, baptising
them into the Name, teaching them to observe ALL things
whatsoever I have commanded you, and, lo, I am with you
—literally—ALL the days, even to the consummation of the
age."

Consider His Power. " All power given to Me . . ."—
anticipating His Ascensiontide coronation. All authority
(exousia, not dunamis) hath been given to Me in Heaven and
on earth! His power! That position our ascended Lord
occupies to-day. All authority in Heaven and on earth is in
the wounded hands of our living Saviour. His power! Ye
fearful saints, fresh courage take!

Consider His Plans. " Go ye therefore . . ."—and this is a
poor translation—with all deference to the divines of 1611—
". . . teaching all nations." No, no: the Revised Version
helps us: " and make disciples of all the nations." But with
infinite respect to them, though that is good English and I
suppose is the best way in which they could put it into an
English translation, still even that is not quite what Jesus said.
For He said, literally, " . . . go and disciple all the nations."
That is His plan: for the nations to be discipled. And He is
doing it! Not that whole nations are ever in this dispensation
to be turned into disciples to a man, but that out of every
nation under Heaven, the Saviour is calling out a people for
His Name. Disciples are to be found in every nation. Notice
that we are to make *disciples*, not converts. A disciple is a
convert consecrated. One real disciple is worth a hundred
mere converts. And disciples have to be made. You can *collect*
converts, but you have to make disciples. And mark the
sequence: " Because of My power on the throne of the
universe in Heaven, you therefore go and disciple the nations
on earth, baptising them. . . ."

Consider His Principles. " Teaching them to observe " (to
guard, to watch over, as the Tomb was guarded) " all things
whatsoever I have commanded you. . . ." The Church is to
give to the nations the principles of Christ—" all things

whatsoever I have commanded you." This would put the world right! But are we Christians observing all, obeying all?

Consider His Presence. " And, lo. I am with you all the days even unto the end." " All the days ",—Sundays and Mondays. All the days! Days of sunshine and ease and holiday—days of thundercloud and turmoil and trial. All the days! Days when everything goes right and days when everything goes wrong. " All the days I am with you." In the Old Tabernacle days at the Saturday night Prayer Meeting we never sang " Standing on the promises " without pausing between each verse and letting folk give a promise that had helped them. And, until they knew better, nearly every time somebody would be bound to quote this verse as a promise: " I am with you always even unto the end of the world." And every time I had to stop them and say: " My dear friend, that is not a promise." I dare say you will find it in your Promise Box, but it is not a promise. He did not say, " I will be with you all the days." It is better than a promise; it is a *fact*! " I am with you always." But even when I have said that, I have not said the greatest thing about it. Perhaps you are familiar with " ego eimi ": the times when the Saviour deliberately does not use the ordinary way of saying " I am " (" eimi " in Greek), but deliberately chooses to use the form whereby He takes the great name for God in the Old Testament on His own lips. This is such a case, and it means nothing less than this: " And, lo, The I AM is with you all the days." So I do not think you ever need be afraid again. The I AM is with you—making no conditions—not saying: " If you do this, that and the other, I will be with you "—but stating a fact, a fact which, as David Livingstone used to say, " is the word of a Gentleman and may be trusted as such ". Jesus says to His own: " I AM with you to the end."

First then, He spoke to the eleven. It is timeless and refers, of course, to other disciples; but it was given to those eleven men of His, the inner circle. And as Mark puts it, He and they working together have been doing it ever since. " The Lord working with them, confirming the word."

II

The second appearance during those forty days is not mentioned in the Gospels at all: for it we are indebted to the Holy Spirit in Paul in 1 Corinthians xv. I refer to the 6th verse. "After that, He was seen of above five hundred brethren at once, of whom the greater part remain unto this present, but some are fallen asleep." Now from that, my friends, I gather that it was the Saviour's wish, somewhen and somewhere in the forty days between Easter and Ascension, to meet all His friends. I imagine that it must have been in Galilee, because on the day of Pentecost in Jerusalem there were only one hundred and twenty of them. The Saviour's widest ministry was in Galilee, and there He made His greatest number of followers. I surmise that on the mountain when He met the eleven He said: " Now I would like to have an informal gathering of all my friends here in Galilee. Send the word round. Bid them come to Me at such-and-such a place at such-and-such a time." And they all came, above five hundred at once.

They are called " brethren ", by which I judge them to be the ordinary rank and file of the Saviour's friends. And the brethren, as often, embrace the sisters! Oh, I would love to have been there! There are few moments in the Saviour's earthly life story at which I would sooner have been present than on this occasion. I wonder who were there. Those three from Bethany would be there surely: Martha and Mary and Lazarus; Lazarus with the unearthly, otherworldly face, the man brought back from the dead; Mary, " Whose eyes were homes of silent prayer "; and Martha, bless her, in charge of the catering if any refreshments were provided. That widow of Nain would be there with that strapping son of hers. They had no charabancs in those days, but I expect they organised parties from different places. Legion—Legion no longer, but he who once was Legion—would surely bring a wagonnette or two from his congregation in Decapolis. Do you think Zaccheus brought a large party from Jericho? Blind Bartimaeus among them, blind no longer. Ah, I wonder if the biggest party of all did not come from Samaria yonder, from that place Sychar, where one woman was used by the Lord to organise so great a revival. I wonder how many ex-lepers were amongst the company! And to make Jesus supremely happy on any such occasion, the children, of course, would be there. Jairus's little daughter, a young madam of about fourteen now—she would be there, and Peter's family, complete with mother-in-law. I wonder if that young couple from Cana were there, probably bringing a little baby with them.

I was over in the Isle of Wight a few years ago for the Baptist Union Assembly there, and at tea I sat next to Dr. Pearce Carey. I had given them a sermon on Wavering Worshippers. He was speaking about this gathering of five hundred brethren at once and said a sweet thing to me. He said, " You know what I like about those five hundred is that they were nearly all young people." I said: " Doctor, where do you get that from? " " Well," he said, " First Corinthians would be written at least thirty years after, and Paul says of that congregation " of whom the greater part remain unto this present, but some are fallen asleep ". Thirty years after Paul says most of them are still alive. In Dr. Pearce Carey's book which he calls by just the one word, " Jesus ", he suggests that it would be to *them* that the Saviour gave the challenge and the commission with which Mark ends his gospel. " Go ye into all the world and preach the gospel to every creature." That is an amplification of the commission given in Matthew xxviii. Dr. Carey says in his book that that is the kind of commission to give to young people. What an ambitious programme for five hundred young disciples of Jesus—" into all the world . . . to every creature—Go! " " Young people " says Dr. Carey, " have been doing that for Jesus ever since."

III

But we must come to the third and last of the appearances we are considering now. If Matthew xxviii's appearance was to the eleven and if the i Corinthians xv. 6 appearance was the five hundred brethren or more, this last appearance was to all the apostles. Now I imagine that to include more than the eleven. I imagine that to include all to whom Jesus had said in the upper room: " As the Father has sent Me, even so send I you." Remember, there is a difference between a disciple and an apostle. A disciple is a learner, a follower of Jesus; an apostle is one definitely sent for a specific work. For His leave-taking Jesus gathered out from among that five hundred, and including the eleven, all whom He regarded as His apostles. I don't think I had better begin to imagine who made up that number! I think we have a glimpse of the same company in the opening chapter of the Acts of the Apostles. His Mother, Mary, is among them; and, by now, His brothers, who before did not believe on Him; the two from Emmaus would be among them; the Apostles, the sent ones, the specially appointed messengers of the living Lord.

For the details of this final leave-taking we are indebted to Luke, partly at the end of his Gospel and partly at the beginning of the sequel to his Gospel which we call " The Acts of the Apostles ". We know from both these accounts where it happened, from whence Jesus ascended to Heaven. I trust I shall not be thought guilty of sentimentality if I spend a few moments lovingly and lingeringly on the fact that Jesus' last spot on earth from which He went back to Heaven was " as far as Bethany ", that is to say, in the Bethany district and on the brow of Olivet.

Now if I had to choose a place for His Ascension I am quite sure I would choose this. On the slopes of Olivet and very near to Bethany. Our Lord, of course, had a great heart and loved the little human touches with which His friends delighted Him; and I am sure it meant much to the Lord to make His way to such a place as Olivet near to Bethany for His final leave-taking. It was so very representative of His earthly life. Memories must have crowded back as He with His disciples made their way through Gethsemane and up the slopes of Olivet towards Bethany. For in this district He had known His greatest joys and His deepest sorrows. Here He had known His truest friends and His basest foes. Here He had been surrounded with love, and here He had been betrayed and forsaken. Bethany, the home where He was happiest, where Martha and Mary and Lazarus had always ready the kiss of welcome, where, as someone puts it so beautifully, He knew "the restfulness of being understood". Bethany! The home perhaps dearest to Him on earth. And Gethsemane, where Judas betrayed His Master with a kiss! So representative of His earthly life. The kiss of welcome and the kiss of treachery. Under these trees He had rested in Mary's garden; under those trees He agonised in Gethsemane. It was here that the crowds started the "Hosannas" on this very road on the way down on Palm Sunday; here the triumphal entry began. Here, in this district, on another path leading into the city, His disciples all forsook Him and fled. Down from here his friends bore Him in triumph singing "Hosanna", cutting down palm branches in His honour; and from here they led Him away with swords and staves and torches. Here He had known His greatest weakness: here He sweated as it were great drops of blood. Here He had known His greatest power: "Lazarus, come forth". So it is here He takes His leave, and from here He ascends. Don't you think that meant much to Him at the time and meant much to them as they thought of it afterwards?

Well, being assembled together they were first of all given the promise of baptism in the Holy Ghost. They are harping, however, on their one dominant string. Listen to them. Even just before He leaves them, they are still going back to the old agitation. "When they therefore were come together, they asked of him saying, 'Wilt Thou at this time restore again the kingdom to Israel?'" They kept on asking, for it is the imperfect—kept on urging the question. It is worth while noticing two things about that in passing. First, that they have regained their confidence in Him now. On the road to Emmaus two of them, voicing the feelings of the rest, said: "We trusted that it had been He which should have redeemed Israel." Meaning that there was no hope of it any longer. They have got back their hope now, for they say: "Lord, wilt Thou *at this time* restore the kingdom? We know that You

are going to do it: are You going to do it *now*? " The second
thing worth noticing in passing is that He never denied that
the kingdom would be restored to Israel. All He said was:
" Mind your own business! " He said, " That is in the Father's
authority. That is for God to say. That is nothing to do with
you." He gently rebuked them. They had been thinking of
that earthly kingdom of temporal glory for years, and to His
pain they are still consumed with interest in *that*. He says in
effect: " Oh yes, that is coming: of course, the kingdom is
going to be restored to Israel "—and, of course, it is. Israel
is yet to come into her own. You tell your Jewish friends
that. You tell them that a day is coming at the Second Advent
when Israel shall come into her own. He *is* going to restore
the Kingdom to Israel and every promise to the Jews is going
to be fulfilled. " But," He says, " that is the Father's business,
and not yours." Some of my extreme and extravagant Second
Adventist friends to-day perhaps need the same rebuke. They
have it all cut and dried for the Father, but the Father does not
want their dates and their plans: it is for ever in His own
authority. " No," says the Saviour just before He leaves them,
" this is to be your business: ye shall receive power, and
having the power, ye shall be My witnesses."

While He was speaking He stretched out His hands in
blessing upon them. " He blessed them." I wonder if He
used the great blessing of the Old Testament, the blessing with
which they would be familiar. " The Lord bless you and keep
you. The Lord make His face shine upon you, and be gracious
unto you. The Lord lift up His countenance upon you and
give you peace." As He blesses, His feet lift from the grass
and, still blessing them He rises upwards. They follow Him
with their gaze, until a cloud intervenes and receives Him out
of their sight. Only out of their sight. Not out of their
company. Only His bodily presence was denied to them.
Had He not said: " Lo, I am with you always "? In a sense,
He did not really go away: He only went out of sight. And
in ten days' time, He was to come to them in a closer way
than ever by His Spirit.

That cloud intrigues me. " Received Him out of " is one

word in the Greek: " to take under." It means to take up by
placing one's self underneath, in the style of a pick-a-back, or
as a waiter holds a tray. It is one of Luke's medical terms.
Dr. Weymouth, always so careful and helpful, puts it thus:
the cloud " closing beneath Him, hid Him from sight ".
Don't tell me that was the sort of cloud which spills the rain
and from which the lightning flashes. No! No! That cloud
was surely a cloud of angelic beings swooping down from
Heaven to bear Him up in triumph to His throne. They came,
says the Greek, and they wrapped Him round, some of them
underneath Him, and into their presence He passed, and the
eyes on earth beheld Him no longer. My own conviction is
that, when at the trump of the archangel we are caught up
with the blessed dead to meet the Lord " in the clouds ", those
clouds will still be clouds of moving beings to meet their
Lord. " Some from earth, from glory some, severed only till
He come." Well, this is surmise, and I cannot prove it. But
the way Luke puts it in the Greek does not suggest an inani-
mate cloud in the sky but a cloud of beings swooping down,
surrounding Him, and bearing Him where no human eye
can follow, into heaven.

Two of that crowd lingered a moment to give a last message
to the upgazing apostles. We always say that it was two *angels*
who came down, but Scripture says " two men ". Why
must they necessarily be angels? Why shouldn't they be two
men? Moses and Elijah came down to the Mount of Trans-
figuration to speak about His exodus. Was it Moses and
Elijah who came down to tell the church of His entry back
into the world? Or, seeing that their message concerned His
Second Advent, would one of the two be Enoch, who pro-
phesied of the Advent, and would the other be Daniel, the
other great Old Testament prophet of the Lord's return?
They may have been angels: if you say they were, I will not
quarrel with you—I only point out to you that Scripture says
" two men ". We will ask about it when we get to the Glory
and we will find out who they were! You know what they
said: " Men, Galileans: why stand ye gazing up into Heaven?
This same Jesus which is taken up from you into Heaven,

shall so come in like manner as ye have seen Him go into Heaven." Could anything be more definite concerning His personal return? And when has this ever yet taken place?

So the message of Ascensiontide is that He occupies the throne; from that throne He gives the Holy Ghost to all who will repent and believe; and just as He ascended, one day from that throne, in like manner, He will descend and His feet shall stand upon the Mount of Olives once again.

CHAPTER SEVEN

JOHN'S EPILOGUE

Reading: John xxi

YOU may wonder why I call this chapter "John's Epilogue" and why I leave it to the end. An epilogue, of course, should come at the end. An epilogue is designed to gather up all that has gone before.

Now it seems quite unquestionable that John wrote this chapter xxi, if I might use such a word of inspired Scripture, as an afterthought. His gospel closes at verse 31 of chapter xx: that is, as you will see, a reasonable, logical, satisfying conclusion to the gospel which has for its object the portraying of our Lord Jesus Christ as God. Then, when John's gospel was finished, the Spirit moved him to take up his pen again and he added this epilogue, the Spirit teaching him that this third appearance to the eleven or their representatives (for only seven of them were present) was in the nature of a summary of all that had gone before, that the reason why Jesus showed Himself like this was to give them something to remember for ever after, as a kind of sweet conclusion to all that He had been saying to them during His ministry.

Where do I get that from? Well, I get it from the word which John uses; and he uses it three times, thus emphasising it. I refer to the word "showed". Verse 1. "After these things Jesus *showed* Himself again . . ." and at the end of the verse "and on this wise *showed* He Himself". Then in verse 14. "This is now the third time that Jesus *showed* Himself to His disciples . . ."

This is not the ordinary word for showing: it does not mean that He just became apparent to them there on the lake shore; it does not mean that He just presented Himself to them again as He had done before. It is an interesting word and a

94

special word. It is a word with two main meanings. The first meaning is to " make visible ", and the suggestion is that Jesus had been there all the time, that He had never left them. Had not He said to them on the mountain of Galilee, " Lo, I am with you always, all the days, even unto the end? " He had never left them. He had been with them: He was there when Simon said, " I go a-fishing "; but the next morning in the grey dawn He made Himself visible to them. He had done it before and He does it now. But the deeper meaning of the word, including that, but going deeper, is to " reveal ". It means that Jesus revealed Himself to them, and the use of the word signifies that it was no ordinary revelation but a special one. Further He revealed *Himself*. The way John puts it again is unusual, calling attention to the fact that Jesus was not just manifested to them, but that He manifested *Himself*. It was His design to reveal Himself to His men in a particularly memorable way, so memorable, and so much summarising everything else that He had revealed about Himself, that John puts it as an epilogue.

You know what happened. Simon Peter and six others went fishing, and Simon Peter was the engineer of it. " I go a-fishing." Well, some think one thing and some another. I can tell you what I think. I think—with a great many others, of course—I think that here is Simon Peter thoroughly disconsolate and very restless and saying to these other six men about him: " Look here, chaps, I can't stand idle any longer: I'm going to get the old boat out." I thoroughly believe that, as on the former occasion when a similar miracle happened, Simon Peter was going back to his old trade. Mind you, we must not be too hard on him, for two reasons. One, because they had not seen Jesus for some time. They were left in the air, as it were. The Saviour had convinced them that He was risen—they did not doubt that for a moment —and He had given them that world commission: " Go ye into all the world and disciple the nations, baptising them, teaching them." Then, presumably, for quite a while they had never seen Him again. Where was He? What were they to do? Oh, He had said to them: " Tarry until you receive the power from on high; " but what could they tell their friends? What were their future movements? It was all uncertain and uncertain at an extraordinarily excitable time, when a man of Peter's temperament would say: " If I've got to evangelise the world, let me get on with it! "

Don't be hard on them for this second reason: it may be that by now their slender resources were giving out. They had given up a prosperous fishing business—four of them, at least—and it may well be that their resources were becoming exhausted; and Peter, presumably thinking that it was an ideal night for fishing, said: " I'm going to get the old boat out." For a second time in his life Peter, having been appointed to be a fisher of men, went back to be a fisherman. I can only surmise that the delay and the absence were because Jesus wanted to wean them away from depending upon His bodily, visible presence, getting them ready for Pentecost when He would be gone for good and they would have the deeper spiritual presence of the Comforter.

So they went fishing. It says: " they entered into a ship ", but it is really " the ship " the old boat—that is the implication: the old boat, Peter's boat. It was a poor show! They went over the waters of Galilee all night long and they took absolutely nothing. " But when the morning was now come, Jesus stood on the shore." It is always morning when Jesus stands on the shore! Just over a hundred yards away from the shore, in the dim light of the breaking day, they discerned a figure on the beach, and a voice came across the water: " Lads! Any food? " Often people would come down early to the sea-shore to buy fish for the markets, when the boats were coming in. They did not waste many words on Him. Each heart knew its own bitterness. They were pretty irritable and disgruntled and disappointed. " No! " Then the voice again from the beach: " Cast the net to starboard; you will find there." That again would give them no surprise because, so I understand, in the half-light of early morning it is possible for a man on the beach to see a shoal of fish in the water that is quite invisible to the fisherman immediately above them in the boat. It may be they had known that to happen before; and I doubt not fairly half-heartedly they flung the net over the other side of the boat. Immediately it tugged and strained and there was a record haul of fish for them. John, with the heart that saw further than the others, is at the side of the boat looking at that figure on the beach, and John is grasping Peter by the arm. "That is the Lord," and Peter grabs his coat about him and flings himself into the sea. And the rest of the men brought in the ship with its load.

How many miracles do you see in this incident? I should be interested to treat you like a Sunday School class for a moment, and say to you: "Hands up those of you who think that in the 21st of John there is one miracle." I wonder how many of you would put your hands up. "How many of you think there are two miracles?" Would your hand go up for that? Then I should like to say: "How many of you think that there are three miracles in this chapter?" Any hands up? Then I should say: "How many of you think that there are *four* miracles in this chapter?" My hand would go up, for one! I believe there are four miracles here, four distinct and separate miracles, and I will proceed to tell you why I think so. Let me clothe my thoughts in almost sermonic fashion, because, remember, this is recorded to teach disciples revealing lessons about their Saviour, summarising what He has been saying to them about their life work, and fixing it on their minds in a way they will not soon or easily forget.

So shall we take as text to-night John's exclamation: "It is the Lord"?

I

HE IS THE LORD OF OUR SERVICE. That is the first thing I believe Jesus intended to teach them from this revelation of Himself. Lord of our service. Here is the first miracle. Unless I am utterly mistaken, the first miracle was that Jesus Christ all night long deliberately kept every fish in Galilee out of their nets. Galilee was so abounding with fish that it was an almost incredible thing that an experienced fisherman could be out all night and catch absolutely nothing. I believe the restraining Hands of the Master of the ocean were keeping fish from their nets. And why? To enforce what He had told them and what they were forgetting: " Without Me ye can do nothing." They had gone back to the old craft without consulting Him. They hadn't prayed about it. Oh, if Peter had been like some church members I know, he would have said glibly: " I prayed about this and the Lord led me to do it." But as events transpire, it was not the Lord leading at all. Reverently, He is not fool enough to do the silly things that some of you do! It is you leading yourself. No, no, He did not send them out. They went without consulting Him, self-led. And He saw to it that they were unsuccessful. He wanted to show them, surely, that, in their future service of fishing for men, without Him it would be " night " and " nothing ". Only by His supreme control could they hope to have any real success.

My friends, that is one of the deepest lessons I have tried to learn in Christian service. Every week I live adds to my conviction of this truth. It is possible for servants of Christ to be busy here and there in His service, to be trying to help Him with His winning of souls in the world and to be doing absolutely nothing for Him. Doing a lot for themselves, but nothing for Him, nothing for eternity. " Night . . . Nothing " you could write over no end of Christian service to-day, and all because it is being done in the energy of the flesh. The Lord is not really being consulted. It is being done for self-centred motives, and The Day will declare of what sort it is.

But I am equally convinced of this: that if I commit my service to Him and go forth in His strength and not my own, and go forth at His behest, obeying His will, with Himself in control, then it is going to be miracle service. There will be His power and blessing upon it. And He will ultimately add the increase. It will be again: " The Lord working with them and confirming the word with signs following." So I believe that all night He kept a catch from their nets and then in the morning flooded their nets with fish by a second miracle to teach them this all-important lesson.

There are other lessons to be learned in this connection. The net was not broken this time. That is miracle number three. Oh, a miracle! Yes, it was impossible for a small boat's net to catch 153 great fishes—for He gave them quality as well as quantity, as Dr. Pearce Carey puts it, " thus finishing off their fishing careers with a fine flourish! "—without the net breaking. Before, in Luke v, the net was torn badly. I wonder if they thought of it afterwards and realised that if the Master is in charge of the service there is no breakdown; but if He is not in charge nets will soon break—nervous breaks—physical breaks—spiritual breaks.

I think this too comes into the first lesson concerning service. Before He called them to breakfast He said: " Now bring all the fish in and count them." He said in effect: " You have gone back to your old craft. I am turning it into an object lesson for the real work to which I have called you. Do you everything decently and in order as I shall always expect it to be done. Bring the net in properly; count them all; don't lay down your task until it is fully and completely done." My dear friends, if He is really the Lord of our service, every bit of it will be done decently and in an orderly manner. Wherever slipshod methods come into church work, wherever workers fail of their task and do it slovenly and shoddily and half-heartedly, it always means one thing: the Lord is not in complete charge. When He is, one way you know it is by every detail being attended to, the whole being done in a way that you know He would have it done. I pause here to ask you this challenging question: Fellow servants of Christ, is He Lord of your service?

II

HE IS THE LORD OF OUR NEEDS. I read on and I find in this gracious chapter the most charming touch of all. What do we find in verse 9? As soon as they were come to land they saw a fire of coals—a fire of charcoal, literally, and fish laid thereon and a loaf. And this is the risen Lord! The Conqueror of death and sin and Satan and hell! The Sovereign, Eternal Master! The One who said to them a few days before, " All authority is given unto Me in Heaven and on earth!" This mighty, mighty Christ has risen early, lit a fire, and is cooking breakfast for half a dozen friends of His. Just like Him!

So I say, secondly, that He is the Lord of our needs. You see the beauty of it. Just precisely what those men needed most in all the world that morning, Jesus had prepared for them. Three things He gave them. They came in cold after being on the chill waters all night, and He had a fire for them. They came in hungry—strong, young, strapping men, out all night working hard though doing nothing, ravenous, and He had a meal for them. They came in irritable, disgruntled, not very pleasant to live with, nervy, moody, Peter like a bear with a sore head, and He gave them fellowship, the charm of His own presence to soothe away their bad temperedness and make them friends again. Just what they needed He had ready for them. "Thou goest before me with the blessings of Thy goodness." I wonder if they thought of that, too. How many times He had said to them: "Don't be anxious about anything. Don't ever let worry harass your mind. God knows all your needs. You are His child and He looks after sparrows and lilies, don't ever let your heart become anxious." Are you trusting Him for even the little things as well as the big things? What a volume of testimony you housewives could compile these days! If the Mistress of the Manse had the time, she could write a book about what she calls her " ravens ". And if in the little things, in the big things too. I believe He wants us to trust Him fully over everything. I believe there is nothing too small to bring in prayer for Him, certainly nothing too great. Only be sure to thank Him for everything.

I would put this word in here because we are living in very dark times and everybody is inclined to nerviness and impatience, and some Christians to-day are getting so irritable that their testimony for Christ is utterly wrecked, almost irreparably wrecked at home and at work, because it is obvious that grace divine within them fails to keep them sweet-tempered. Ah, it is just then that we need to live nearer to Jesus than ever, and in the enjoyment of His fellowship we

shall be kept sweet and kind and calm. Lord of our Needs!
Yes, every time He is trusted.

III

HE IS THE LORD OF OUR WORSHIP. This was
no ordinary meal. Will you look at verses 12 and 13? " Jesus
said unto them, ' Come and dine'. And none of the disciples
ventured to ask Him ' Who art Thou' knowing it was the
Lord. Jesus then cometh and taketh *a* loaf and giveth them
and *a* fish likewise." It is the diminutive for fish, a little fish,
the same way as John puts it in the feeding of the five
thousand: " five barley loaves and two small fishes,"—little
dabs or something of that sort. One loaf and one small fish
to feed eight hungry young men for breakfast! Then here is
the fourth miracle, obviously. They are taken again in thought
to the green downs of Galilee when the five thousand were
fed, followed the next day by that discourse on the bread of
life. Here again the Lord is serving them with miracle bread
multiplied in His hands. And there is a wondrous awe and
stillness upon them. Even Peter has nothing to say. The meal
becomes a sacrament. It takes them also to the upper room.
It savours of that communion service when He broke the
bread and gave it to them. He is doing it again. And they
worship. There seems to have been a hush over the meal—
that " deep hush, subduing all our words and works ". Even
Peter has nothing to say.

Now I value having the second and the third in such close
association. On the one hand, I want to trust Him as my
dearest Friend who will take a divine interest in the littlest
things of my life; but, on the other hand, I want to keep in my
heart the awe and adoration that befits the mighty, eternal
Christ of God. I speak especially to you young people. You
know, it is so easy to get too familiar with Jesus Christ. I
have sometimes had to pull some of you up, as you know.
You say glibly and irreverently " The Lord this " and " The
Lord that "; " The Lord told me to do this " and " The Lord
told me to do that." Well, that is all very well, but it is

possible, in becoming too familiar with Christ, to treat Him only as a Companion upon the road and to forget that He is the everlasting Lord upon the Throne. I would fain keep ever in my own heart this stillness, this worshipfulness, this quiet adoration as He broke the sacramental food and miraculously distributed to them in the opening light of the early morning. Lord of our Service! Lord of our Needs! Lord of our Worship!

IV

HE IS THE LORD OF OUR LOVE. The meal is over now and Simon Peter is drawn on one side. Then that searching question thrice repeated: " Simon, Son of Jonas, lovest thou Me? " In that way the Lord had addressed Peter the first time they ever met, when Andrew brought him. It was then he had been surnamed Peter. " Thou art Simon, the son of Jonas; thou shall be called ' Rock '." The first time (on this occasion) you remember, it was, " Simon, lovest thou Me more than these? " Simon, you have gone back to the old boat. You have become a fisherman again. For the second time since I called you, you have left My appointed service of fishing for men and you have gone back to that boat. Simon, I know you love it. I know that you left a big all when you left that craft to follow Me. Simon, if you are going to be of any use to Me in the coming days, your usefulness stands or falls by this: do you really love Me? Do you love Me *more* than those things of the old life before I called you? And Simon Peter was able to satisfy the heart of his Lord; and the Lord was able to gratify Simon Peter by entrusting him with the feeding of the lambs and the shepherding of the sheep in coming days.

You are familiar with the two words for love here: the Saviour's superlative word and Peter's lesser word. The English translation makes the word " love " serve for both. Peter's grief the third time was not that his Lord pressed the query three times, but because the third time He descended to Peter's lesser word. But still Peter could not bring himself to use of his poor love the Master's lofty term. His deep consolation lay in this: " Lord, Thou knowest! "

But what about that charcoal fire? Charcoal is not the ordinary fuel in Eastern lands. Charcoal is very difficult to get burning and only once else in the New Testament do we read of charcoal being used for a fire. That other time was, significantly enough, on Good Friday morning, when, in the chill of breaking day in the courtyard of the High Priest's palace the enemies of Christ lit a fire to warm themselves, at which fire Peter warmed himself and by the glowing embers of which his own heart's fire all but died and he denied his Lord. Now burning charcoal has a peculiarly pungent tang, and you know how an aroma has the power to quicken memory. You have all somewhere breathed in a perfume, your mind instantly going back through the years and recalling vividly an experience long bygone. I cannot help feeling that Jesus deliberately chose charcoal as fuel that morning for Simon Peter's benefit; and that may be what kept him so quiet. The reek of the pungent charcoal was in his nostrils, bringing back to him the last time he had smelt charcoal burning. It was in searching mood of that memory that Jesus took him aside to challenge him about his love.

Is He Lord of your love? Our victory and radiance in the daily living of the Christian life depend upon our personal devotion to Him. Our real success in Christian service and testimony stands or falls according to whether or not we really love Jesus, and whether or not we really love Him more than other things, and other people—and self. Do you? And we only love Him at all because He first loved us!

V

HE IS THE LORD OF OUR DEPARTURE. As I come to the end of this chapter, I find His Lordship in one other matter: in the realm of death. " Verily, verily, I say unto thee, when thou wast young, thou girdedst thyself, and walkedst whither thou wouldest; but when thou shalt be old, thou shalt stretch forth thine hands and another shall gird thee, and carry thee whither thou wouldest not. This spake He signifying by what manner of death he should glorify God. And when He had spoken this, He saith unto him, Follow Me." Yes, Peter, you are going to die by crucifixion, you are going to die a martyr; but I know all about it. It is in My hands. And Peter banked on it at the time of supreme peril. When Herod, having beheaded James, took Peter also, to win more favour with the Jews, and kept him closely guarded during Passover week, intending after Easter to put him to death as a public spectacle, Peter, on his last night before what seemed like inevitable martyrdom, slept so soundly between his guards that the angel had to smite him to waken him; and so deep was his slumber that the angel dared not leave him on his own until they were half across the city! Why such sleep in such a plight? His Master had said, " *When thou shalt be old* ": so he knew he would be delivered somehow and slept like a child.

" And what shall this man do? " " Never mind that man. If I will that he tarry till I come, that is not your business. You travel along with Me yourself. However you die, either of you, I am Lord of your departure. The death of My servants is not out of My own control." Nor is it. Please God I hope to tarry till He come, not to die at all, but whether that or the usual lowering into the grave matters nothing: He who was the Lord at my beginning will be the Lord at my ending. In that quiet certainty Peter and John—Peter to crucifixion, John to ripe old age, in the nineties or over—and any of us, can quietly travel along with Him. He will be with us to the end and in the end and beyond the end.

So there is John's epilogue. Isn't it lovely? Doesn't it give us a summary of what Jesus has said one way or another during the whole of His ministry? Isn't it a foretaste of the Morning? Aren't we now toiling in the sea and isn't He standing on the eternal shore and isn't the morning coming for each of His own when He is going to make Himself visible to us, when He is going to call us to Himself, when He is going to say, " Bring of the fish which ye have now caught "? Are you going to have some to bring? Are you going to be able to step on to the shore of eternity and meet His smile with some converts of yours? Or as yet haven't you one fish to bring with you that you have caught? He will be disappointed and so will you. As Paul says to his converts: " Are ye not our hope and joy and crown of rejoicing in the presence of our Lord Jesus? " There are some of you to whom in God's infinite goodness, I am spiritual father; I have caught you in the gospel net and I am going to take you to my Saviour that morning. You will be glad to come with me. Then He is going to call us to breakfast. He is getting it ready now—that wondrous meal when every church member will be present. And He has said: " Verily I say unto you, He shall gird Himself and make them to sit down to meat and will come forth and serve them." And I think it will take all eternity to tell Him how much we really love Him.